golf's
all-time firsts, mosts, leasts, and a few nevers

golf's
all-time firsts, mosts, leasts, and a few nevers

Al Barkow

TAYLOR TRADE PUBLISHING
Lanham • New York • Boulder • Toronto • Plymouth, UK

Published by TAYLOR TRADE PUBLISHING
An imprint of The Rowman & Littlefield Publishing Group, Inc.
4501 Forbes Boulevard, Suite 200, Lanham, Maryland 20706
www.rlpgtrade.com

Estover Road, Plymouth PL6 7PY, United Kingdom

Distributed by National Book Network

British Library Cataloguing in Publication Information Available

Library of Congress Cataloging-in-Publication Data
Barkow, Al.
 Golf's all-time firsts, mosts, leasts, and a few nevers / Al Barkow.
  p. cm.
 ISBN 978-1-58979-676-8 (pbk. : alk. paper) — ISBN 978-1-58979-677-5
(electronic)
 1. Golf—Miscellanea. 2. Golf—Records. I. Title.
 GV967.B313 2012
 796.352—dc23

                                        2011044433

⊗™ The paper used in this publication meets the minimum requirements of
American National Standard for Information Sciences—Permanence of Paper
for Printed Library Materials, ANSI/NISO Z39.48-1992.

Printed in the United States of America

contents

introduction

G olfers are no different from those who follow other sports in America. We all love statistics—the who, the what, the when, the where, and the how many. It's information that is comforting, that brings some order in a world often ringing of chaos and uncertainty. Facts are solid, irrefutable, and that's one reason we go for them. But there is also a historical component. It's nice to know events don't just happen out of the blue, are not once in a lifetime but part of a continuum. That's why a good many of the entries in this book include the how and why. We all like yarns, backgrounders, and the context in which significant and even insignificant events take place. Some flesh is put on the bare bones of numbers, dates, and names.

But to not get too carried away with monumental purpose, let me say that there is also a fun element involved. I think it's kind of neat to know why the founders of the Myopia Golf Club named it that. And why the Nassau Golf Club created a scoring system that turned into golf's most popular betting game. It's not stuff we need to know, but it's nice information to have anyway.

There is a certain organization to the presentation of this material, but it is not strictly structured. I thought the best way to give the collection some order was to break it up into major golf organizations and their events, and within them the specifics—the Firsts, Mosts, and Leasts. But there are special sections, such as Women's Golf, and my favorite, Miscellaneous. The thing I like about this sort of makeup is that, as you browse the pages, you come up with surprises. You might also use it for a game of Golf Jeopardy. This is a book that in its structure is meant to be browsed. So, good browsing to you.

—Al Barkow

1 united states golf association championships

THE US OPEN,
US AMATEUR,
ETC.

▶ FIRSTS

First US Open, **1895**, at Newport CC, Rhode Island. It was won by Horace Rawlings, an immigrant Englishman, with rounds of 91–82. It originated as a thirty-six-hole event.

First US Open (at Seventy-two Holes), **1898**, at Myopia Hunt Club, Hamilton, Massachusetts. Fred Herd won it with rounds of 84–85–75–84 on a nine-hole course they played eight times in two days. **The club's name derived from the fact that the four brothers who founded it had poor vision.* This was also the *First Time the US Open Was Played at a Course Separate from the US Amateur Championship Course.*

First Four-Time and Back-to-Back Winner of the US Open, **Willie Anderson**, who won in 1901, 1903, 1904, and 1905.

First (and Only) Winner of a Faux US Open, **Ben Hogan**, 1942, at Ridgemoor CC, Chicago. Faux because the official US Open had been cancelled for the duration of World War II. Jack Kelly, father of movie star Grace Kelly, devised this event, named the Hale America National Open. He was a physical fitness devotee—hence the Hale in the title—and used the event to raise money for the Navy Relief Society and the USO (United Service Organization). Ben Hogan, to his dying day, noting the word *National* in the title of this tournament and the design of the front side of the medal he received, counted it as his fifth US Open victory. He further argued his case by reminding everyone that the tournament was sponsored by the United States Golf Association, which stages the official US Open. However, the Hale America was also sponsored by the PGA of America and the Chicago District Golf Association. Furthermore, the medal mentioned above signifies that it was the Hale America National Open Golf Tournament, not Championship, which is how all official USGA events are termed. Finally, the venue was not at all up to US Open standards in terms of difficulty. It played at 6,519 yards, and Hogan's winning score of 271 was 17 under par. The lowest winning score in the US Open up to that time was 281, and in the next two official renewals was 284 and 282. So, faux.

First Homebred American to Win the US Open, **Johnny McDermott**, 1911. McDermott successfully defended the title in 1912 to become the *First Homebred Back-to-Back Winner of the Championship*. McDermott was from the Philadelphia area and had a mercurial, and in the end rather sad, even tragic, life following his victories. He was a brilliant championship golfer between 1912 and 1914, having won not only the US Opens but also the Western Open, a major title in that time, and three Philadelphia Opens. However, after defeating Harry Vardon and Ted Ray to win the 1913 Shawnee Open (just as Francis Ouimet did that year in the 1913 US Open, which of course received far more notice), McDermott made some comments publicly that was construed as rudely boastful. He apologized after being roundly criticized, but he felt privately that his remarks were misunderstood. He lost considerable money with poor investments in that period. Then, in 1914 he entered the British Open but arrived too late to play. He booked a ship home, but shortly after the ship set sail it collided with another vessel and had to return to port, in England. McDermott was put aboard another ship the next day and made it home, but it seemed he never got over the loss of money, the embarrassment of his remarks at Shawnee, and the dangers of the collision at sea. Not long after returning to the United States he blacked out while entering the clubhouse of the Atlantic City CC, where he was the professional, and from that day on he spent the rest of his life in mental institutions, rest homes, and living in his parent's home. He never played golf again, and he died at the age of 80. He was not entirely forgotten, though. At the 1971 US Open, at the Merion Golf Club, just outside Philadelphia, McDermott attended for a day. Almost no one recognized him, except Arnold Palmer, who greeted him warmly and praised his accomplishments. A few months later, McDermott died.

First to Break 70 in the US Open, **Dave Hunter**, 1909, with a 68 in the first round, at the Englewood GC in New Jersey. He had an 84 in the second round and eventually a seventy-two-hole total of 313, 23 off the winning pace, to tie for 31st.

First to Break 80 in All Four Rounds of the US Open, **Laurie Auchterlonie**, 1902, at the Garden City GC, New York, with rounds of 78–78–74–77. He won by six shots.

The First Winner of the US Open Using the Haskell Ball, **Laurie Auchterlonie**, 1902. Auchterlonie used the then new three-piece, rubber-core ball, called the Haskell after its inventor, Coburn Haskell, which was far livelier than the solid gutta-percha ball that was played for the past fifty years or so. The Haskell, also called unofficially the "Bounding Billie" because it gave up so much more roll after landing, had a solid core wound with rubber bands and was covered with balata. It was the proto-type of all golf balls from that time until the one- and two-piece Surlyn-covered golf ball was developed in the 1960s. (See more under **Equipment**.)

First to Break 300 in the US Open, **Alex Smith**, in 1906, at the Onwentsia Club, Lake Forest, Illinois. He had 295 on rounds of 73–74–73–75. No par for the course was registered.

First to Break 65 in a US Open Round, **Lee Mackey**, with a 64 in the first round of the 1950 Championship, at Merion GC, Ardmore, Pennsylvania. He followed that magical round with an 81, then shot rounds of 75–77 to finish in a tie for 25th.

First Wire-to-Wire Winner of the US Open, **Walter Hagen**, 1914, at Midlothian CC, outside Chicago. It was affirmation of the adage, or warning, "Beware the athlete who comes off the sick bed." Hagen was in the process of overcoming a case of food poisoning after eating a tainted lobster.

First Winner of the US Open in a Playoff, **Willie Anderson**, 1901, at the Myopia Hunt Club, Huntington, Massachusetts. He defeated Alex Smith, 85 to 86.

First US Amateur Champion, **Charles Blair MacDonald**, 1895, at Newport GC, Rhode Island. In the final match MacDonald defeated Charles Sands by a score of 12 and 11. Actually, it was the second national amateur championship. The first was in 1894, but MacDonald finished second and afterward complained that the tournament was run so poorly it didn't count. A strong personality (read egotist), MacDonald gathered together some other gentlemen golfers and golf clubs and founded the United States Golf Association in 1895. The Amateur championship held that year was won by MacDonald, who was now satisfied that he was in fact, by his lights, the best golfer in the nation.

While he was quite full of himself, MacDonald did contribute significantly to the game. He designed a number of courses that to this day are highly regarded; they include the National Golf Links, on Long Island, New York, and *The First Eighteen-Hole Golf Course in the United States,* the **Chicago Golf Club,** which opened for play at 6,500 yards in 1894.

First to Score All Four Rounds in the 60s in the US Open, **Lee Trevino,** 1968, at Oak Hill CC, Rochester, New York. His rounds were 69–68–69–69 for a winning score of five-under par 275. Jack Nicklaus was second at 279.

First to Score Four Sub-Par Rounds in the US Open, **Sam Snead,** 1947. However, it took Sam five rounds to do it; he was one-over par (72) in the first round, then had 70–70–70 in regulation play, and another 70 in the playoff, which he lost to Lew Worsham's 69.

First (and So Far Only) Former US Open Champion to be Forcibly Disqualified from a Tournament, **Cyril Walker.** Walker, winner of the 1924 US Open, was a notoriously slow player—owing at least in part, according to contemporaries, to his problems with alcohol consumption. According to Paul Runyan, in the book *Gettin' to the Dance Floor: An Oral History of American Golf,* at the fifth hole during his first round in the 1930 Los Angeles Open, Walker was asked by two policemen, instructed by the tournament officials, to speed up his play. Angered, he became abusive and said to the law men, "Who the hell are you? I'm a US Open champion," adding that he had traveled three thousand miles to play in this diddy-bump tournament and would play as slow as he damn well pleased. When he got to the ninth hole he was told he was disqualified. He replied, "The hell I am. I came here to play, and I'm going to play." At that, the two police officers picked him up by the elbows (Walker was a tiny man, weighing around 120 pounds) and carried him away. "I can still see him being carried up the hill," Runyan recalled many years later, "kicking his legs like a banty rooster. They threw him off the course and told him not to come back or he'd go to the pokey."

First to Make the US Open a First Victory as a Professional, Jack Fleck, 1955, at the Olympic GC, San Francisco, in a playoff with Ben Hogan. This also qualifies as a *Most* by being, perhaps, *The Biggest Upset Winner of the US Open.* (See elsewhere in this book.)

First Regional Qualifying for the US Open, 1924. This was a reflection of the growing interest in golf in the United States. Qualifying had always been held at the site of the championship itself. But the number of entries had expanded enough to require qualifying at different locations. In this case, at Oak Park, Illinois, and Worcester, Massachusetts, to get to Detroit for the main event.

First Army "Brat" to Win the US Amateur and US Open, Lawson Little, whose doctor father made his career in the US Army. Little developed his game as a youngster playing on the Presidio Golf Course in San Francisco, which is now a public course but back then was restricted to military personnel. Little wasn't really a brat; he was an intelligent, well-mannered person, a superb player, and a credit to the game.

First Under-Par Winner of the US Open, Johnny McDermott, 1912, with 294* at the Country Club of Buffalo (New York).

*A high number to be under par, by current standards, but according to the USGA Record Book, in 1911 the term *par* first came into official usage and was defined as "perfect play without flukes and under ordinary weather conditions, always allowing two strokes on each putting green." Pretty vague, because a par-4 on a day of low to no winds might be a par-5 if the weather is lousy. And a "fluke" was never defined. It wasn't until 1923 when the USGA began to designate exact yardages to determine the par of a hole, no matter the conditions. It was generally considered that a par-3 was up to 175 yards in length, a par-4 from 176 to 450 yards long (although there were few if any par-4s under 250 yards long), and a par-5 anything over 450 yards. The numbers have been gradually increased, at least for the pros, in light of the distances that modern technology allows them to hit the ball. (See entry on **First Use of Par**, in **Miscellaneous.**)

First Teenager to Win the US Open, **Johnny McDermott,** 1911, at the Chicago Golf Club. He was 19 years, 10 months.

First Winner of the US Open and PGA Championship in the Same Year, **Gene Sarazen,** 1922.

First (and Only) Doctor to Win the US Open (and the Masters), **Dr. Cary Middlecoff,** 1949. He practiced dentistry in Memphis for a couple of years before opting to play professional golf. He won the US Open again in 1956, the Masters in 1955, and, in all, thirty-nine tournaments during a long and illustrious career. The only other trained doctor to play professional golf was (and is) Gil Morgan, an optometrist.

First Player to Score Under 280 Twice in the US Open and Not Win, **Arnold Palmer.** In 1966 he tied Billy Casper at 278 and lost in a playoff, and in 1967, with a 279, lost by four strokes to Jack Nicklaus.

First Amateur to Win the US Open, **Francis Ouimet,** 1913, at The Country Club, in Brookline, Massachusetts, in a famous playoff and astounding upset against the two best professionals in the game at the time—Englishmen Harry Vardon and Ted Ray. The victory is generally acknowledged to have given golf in America its first real boost in general interest.

First Amateur to Win Both the US Open and US Amateur in the Same Year, **Charles "Chick" Evans,** 1916. Evans, from Chicago, is one of the premier amateur champions in American golf history. A dedicated amateur, after his success in the Open and Amateur he earned royalties from recordings of golf instruction. If he accepted the money for his personal use he would have lost his amateur status, and at the suggestion of his mother he diverted the money to create the Evans Scholarship Foundation, which exists to this day and provides four-year university scholarships to young people from the caddie ranks who have demonstrated need for this financial help, have a good grade average, and are of good character. It was *The First Caddie Scholarship Program* and has, since 1930, when it began, provided over ten thousand scholarships. It has also spawned numerous similar programs throughout the country.

First Playoff for a US Open, **1901,** Willie Anderson and Alex Smith. Both finished the regulation seventy-two holes with 331. The score is not related to par, as there was no such designation at the time. (Again, see entry on **First Use of Par,** in **Miscellaneous.**)

First US Amateur Championship Played West of the Mississippi, **1921,** at St. Louis CC, Clayton, Missouri. It was won by Jesse Guilford, who defeated Robert Gardner in the final.

First US Open Played West of the Mississippi River, **1938,** at the Cherry Hills Club, Denver, Colorado. It was won by Ralph Guldhal, who won by six strokes in his successful defense of the title.

First US Amateur Played West of the Rocky Mountains, **1929,** at Pebble Beach Golf Links, Pebble Beach, California and Del Monte G&CC. The winner was Harrison Johnston, from Minnesota.

Note: The above three geographic notations are made because the USGA was, in its earliest years, accused of being an East Coast "clique" with little interest in spreading the national championships around the country.

First US Publinks Champion, **Edmund Held**, 1922, at Ottawa Park GC, Toledo, Ohio. This entry relates to the three above in that this championship was meant to ameliorate the widely held feeling that the USGA was an elitist organization interested only in golf played at private golf clubs. On these grounds, James Standish, of Detroit, persuaded the Committee to inaugurate a championship exclusively for public-fee golfers, and he donated a cup to serve as a perpetual trophy. It was a great success for a start-up, with 140 entrants and 136 starters who tried to qualify over thirty-six holes for the thirty-two match-play spots.

An odd but mentionable aside: While surely not related to the event in any way, during one of the matches a pistol shot was heard at the back of the gallery. It happened that a gentleman decided at that time to take his life. This may qualify for being *The First Suicide by a Spectator at a National Championship.* The name is withheld to protect the privacy of surviving family, heirs, etc.

First US Junior Amateur Championship, **1948**. Dean Lind defeated Ken Venturi in the final, at the University of Michigan Golf Course. There were 495 entries in this inaugural.

First Public Course to Host a US Open Qualifier, St. Andrews GC, in Lemont, Illinois, 1947. It was meet and proper that this first should be at a course owned and operated by Joe Jemsek, the country's premier public course owner/operator.

First International Golfer to Win the US Amateur, **C. Ross "Sandy" Somerville**, a Canadian, 1932.

First American Winner of the US Amateur Who Did Not Wear a Jacket, **Jerome Travers**, 1907. Harry Vardon modified the jackets in which he played, using a straight razor to cut under the arms. The idea was picked up by a tailor, who invented the pleated armhole for golf jackets. The tailor was behind the curve, however, as the wearing of jackets by almost all golfers soon went out of fashion.

First American Winner of the US Open Who Did Not Wear a Jacket, **Francis Ouimet**, 1913. Both Harry Vardon and Ted Ray, whom Ouimet defeated in the playoff, did wear jackets.

First Handicap System, **1905**. The USGA introduced the Calkins system as a basis for determining the eligibility of entrants to the US Amateur Championship. This relates to the creation of the par, as noted later.

First Hole-in-One in the US Open, **Jack Hoben**, 1907. On the 147-yard 10th hole at the Philadelphia Cricket Club. Hoben finished 4th in the championship.

FIRST WINNERS OF THE US OPEN, BY STATE BORN IN

First from Alabama, **Hubert Green**, 1977. Notable Others: Jerry Pate (1976), Larry Nelson (1983).

First from California, **Olin Dutra**, 1934. Notable Others: Lawson Little (1940), Ken Venturi (1964), Billy Casper (1959, 1966), Gene Littler (1961), Johnny Miller (1973), Scott Simpson (1987), Corey Pavin (1995), Tiger Woods (2000, 2002, 2008).

First from Connecticut, **Billie Burke**, 1931. Notable Others: Dick Mayer (1957), Julius Boros (1952, 1963).

First from Georgia, **Bobby Jones**, 1923.

First from Illinois, **Charles "Chick" Evans**, 1916.

First from Indiana, **Frank Urban "Fuzzy" Zoeller**, 1984.

First from Iowa, Jack Fleck, 1955.

First from Kansas, Hale Irwin, 1974.

First from Massachusetts, Francis Ouimet, 1913.

First from Minnesota, Lee Janzen, 1993.

First from Missouri, Tom Watson, 1982. Notable Others: Payne Stewart (1991, 1999).

First from Nebraska, Johnny Goodman, 1933.

First from New Mexico, Steve Jones, 1996.

First from New York, Walter Hagen, 1914. Notable Others: Jerome Travers (1915), Johnny Farrell (1928), Gene Sarazen (1922, 1932), Tony Manero (1936), Craig Wood (1941).

First from North Carolina, Raymond Floyd, 1986.

First from Ohio, Jack Nicklaus, 1962 (1967, 1972, 1980).

First from Oklahoma, Tommy Bolt, 1958. Notable Others: Orville Moody (1969).

First from Pennsylvania, John McDermott, 1911. Notable Others: Sam Parks (1935), Arnold Palmer (1960), Jim Furyk (2003).

First from South Carolina, Lucas Glover, 2009.

First from Tennessee, Cary Middlecoff, 1948. Notable Others: Lou Graham (1975).

First from Texas, Ralph Guldahl, 1937 (1938). Notable Others: Ben Hogan (1948, 1950, 1951, 1953), Byron Nelson (1939), Lloyd Mangrum (1946), Lee Trevino (1968, 1971), Tom Kite (1992).

First from Virginia, Lew Worsham, 1947. Notable Others: Curtis Strange (1988, 1989).

First from Wisconsin, Andy North, 1978 (1985).

⚌ FIRST INTERNATIONAL WINNERS OF THE US OPEN, BY NATIVE COUNTRY

First Englishman, **Horace Rawlins,** 1895.

First Scotsman, **Jim Foulis,** 1896.

First South African, **Gary Player,** 1965.

First Australian, **David Graham,** 1981.

First Argentinean, **Angel Cabrera,** 2007.

First Irishman, **Graeme McDowell,** 2010.

First to Reach 13, 14, 15, 16, and 17 Under Par in a US Open, **Rory McIlroy,** 2011.

First Admission Charged to Witness a US Open, **1922,** at the Skokie CC, outside Chicago. Charge, $1.

First Left-Hander to Win the US Amateur, **Phil Mickelson,** 1990.

First Left-Hander to Make the Cut in the US Open, **Loddie Kempa,** 1948.

First to Win the US Amateur Championship and the NCAA Individual Title in the Same Year, **Jack Nicklaus,** 1961.

The First Walker Cup Match, **1922.** The competition between the best US and British amateurs preceded the Ryder Cup Match by five years; even more, given its gestation history. Begun in the wake of World War I with a view to stimulating golf interest on both sides of the Atlantic Ocean, the concept was born in 1919 when the Royal Canadian Golf Association invited the USGA to send an amateur team to Canada. A ten-man squad that included such all-stars as Bobby Jones, "Chick" Evans, and Francis Ouimet, defeated the Canadians 12–3 at the Hamilton (Ontario) GC. The

US team won a return match the following year, 10–4, at the Engineers CC, in New York.

At the same time, top British and American amateur golfers were competing in each country's national amateur championships, which brought together committee members from the USGA and R&A. Between them another international team competition, similar to that which took place in Canada, was conceived. Among the American participants was George Herbert Walker, president of the USGA, a low-handicap golfer out of St. Louis who very much liked the idea. In December 1920, Walker presented a plan for the competition and offered to donate a cup to symbolize it. He called it the International Challenge Trophy, but space-challenged newspapers began calling it the Walker Cup, to Mr. Walker's chagrin. But the name stuck, and the competition went forward. Walker, by the way, was a grandfather of George Herbert Walker Bush, the 41st president of the United States.

First Father and Son to Make the Cut in a US Open, **Joe Kirkwood Sr. and Joe Kirkwood Jr.,** 1948.

First Use of Gallery Ropes, **1954,** at the Baltusrol GC, Springfield, New Jersey. The idea was proposed by Robert Trent Jones Sr. It reflected the growth of attendance in American golf and the need to control it. Previously, galleries were allowed to follow the golfers in the fairways.

First US Senior Open, **1980.** Won by Roberto DeVicenzo, at Winged Foot CC, Mamaroneck, New York. He shot 285 on the East Course. Amateur Bill Campbell was runner-up, at 289.

▷ MOSTS

States Producing Most US Open Champions, **Texas and California,** with eleven each.

Longest Playoff in US Open (and Golf History), **Seventy-two holes,** to conclude the 1931 championship. At the Inverness Club, in Toledo, Ohio, George Von Elm and Billy Burke played another seventy-two-hole tournament to decide the winner of the first seventy-two holer. When Von Elm birdied the 72nd hole of regulation play, he tied with Burke at 292 (+8). The USGA was then using a thirty-six-hole playoff format in case of a tie, but Von Elm and Burke tied for that at 149 (+6) when Von Elm once again holed for a birdie on the last hole. Von Elm, a Californian who had played most of his golf as an amateur—and a very good one—defeated Bobby Jones in the final of the 1926 US Amateur, and then turned pro. He couldn't quite keep up his miracles, however. Burke went a stroke up with five holes to play and held on to win, 148–149. It was the last year the USGA used a thirty-six-hole playoff system. It went to eighteen holes, but another eighteen if there was a tie after the first one, and so on. Finally, the USGA more or less joined the modern age and altered its playoff system, retaining the eighteen-hole playoff but going to sudden death if the players are still tied.

Most US Open Victories, **Four,** by Bobby Jones, Ben Hogan, and Jack Nicklaus.

Most US Open Victories by an Amateur, **Four**, Bobby Jones.

Oldest Winner of the US Open, **Hale Irwin,** who was 45 years and 15 days old when he won the 1990 championship, at Medinah CC outside Chicago.

Oldest to Make the Cut in the US Open, **Sam Snead**, in the 1973 championship, at Oakmont CC. He was 61, and finished tied for 29th.

Biggest Lead Lost in Last Round of a US Open, **Seven strokes**, by Mike Souchak in the 1960 championship at the Cherry Hills CC in Denver. And, by Arnold Palmer in the 1966 championship at the Olympic Club in San Francisco.

Souchak shot a 75 (+4) in his last round, while Palmer shot a stirring, historic 65 (–6) to overtake Souchak and win by two over Jack Nicklaus, who was still an amateur. Souchak finished tied for third.

Ironically, in 1966 Palmer lost the seven-shot lead he held through sixty-three holes, shooting a 39 on the back nine to Billy Casper's 32. Casper won the eighteen-hole playoff, again coming from behind—two shots after nine holes—to beat Palmer 69 to 73.

Biggest or Most Astounding Upset in US Open (if Not All of Golf) History, **Francis Ouimet defeating Harry Vardon and Ted Ray in a playoff for the 1913 championship;** *Or,* **Jack Fleck defeating Ben Hogan in a playoff for the 1955 title.** Take your pick.

Ouimet was a 20-year-old amateur with limited competitive achievements, and those were only around his home state of Massachusetts. Vardon was by all accounts, and by his record, the best golfer in the world at the time and was still in his prime. Ray was generally considered World Number Two. Yet, at The Country Club, in Brookline, Massachusetts, across the road from where Ouimet lived, the youngster outdueled the two pros over eighteen extra holes with a 72 to Vardon's 77 and Ray's 78.

Ouimet's victory has long been hailed as the event that gave golf its first big boost in interest in the United States.

Jack Fleck, age 32, was a nondescript golf professional who operated two municipal golf courses in Davenport, Iowa. During the winter months he had made a few unimpressive forays on the pro tour and in national championships. He had no record of achievement to speak of. Ben Hogan, of course, was one of the greatest golfers the game had ever had. Two years earlier he had completed the so-called Tri-Slam, winning the Masters, the US

Open, and in his only effort ever, the British Open. It appeared almost certain he would capture his fifth US Open title at the Olympic Club in 1955. It was a goal he had long sought, to be the only player to win the title five times. And indeed, he finished at 287 and had been congratulated on radio as the winner by Gene Sarazen. Others did the same in the locker room. Prematurely, but understandably. The only person still on the course with any chance of catching Hogan was Fleck, and no one gave him a chance. But Fleck birdied two of the last four holes of regulation play and forced an eighteen-hole playoff.

Hogan, who somehow was not as good in playoffs as might be expected, never led in the eighteen-hole playoff. To be sure, he was playing on aching legs, which had taken a heavy toll playing on soft turf and in the heavy, moist air of the seaside course on the western edge of San Francisco. The strain was even greater given that the day before he had played the last thirty-six regulation holes, which at that time was the format for the Open. Still, he was Ben Hogan playing someone named Fleck.

After ten holes Hogan trailed by three strokes, but he did close the gap and was only a stroke behind with one hole to play. However, his foot slipped on the heavily sanded 18th tee and he pulled his drive badly into the knee-high rough on the left. It took him two shots just to get out of the rough, and although he holed a miraculous downhill forty-foot putt for a double-bogey six, it was not enough. Fleck won, 69–72. Ironically, or perhaps fittingly, Fleck was using clubs made by the then new Ben Hogan Golf Company and which Hogan had given him at no charge. Fleck was the only pro using them, except for Hogan.

Largest Winning Margin in the US Open, **Twelve strokes**, by Tiger Woods, in the 1997 championship at Pebble Beach Golf Links, California.

Largest Winning Margin in Final of the US Amateur Champion-ship, **12 & 11**, by Charles Blair MacDonald over Charles Sands, in 1895 (the inaugural).

Tallest Winner of the US Open, **Andy North**, at 6'4". North won the 1978 and 1985 US Opens.

Oldest Winner of the US Amateur Championship, **Jack West-land**, 47 years, 8 months, 9 days, in 1952.

Most Strokes Taken on a Par-3 in the US Open, **Eighteen**, by Willie Chisholm, in the 1919 championship. It was on the 185-yard 8th hole at Brae Burn CC, West Newton, Massachusetts. Chisholm's first shot came up against a boulder. Rather than take an unplayable lie penalty he took chips out of the boulders and got his name in the record book.

Most Strokes Taken on Any Hole in a US Open, **Nineteen**, by Ray Ainsley in 1938, at the par-4 16th hole of the Cherry Hills CC, Englewood, Colorado. He tried to play out of a creek.

Longest Last Name of a US Open Winner, **Auchterlonie**, Laurie, with twelve letters.

Most Second-Place Finishes in the US Open, **Five**, by Phil Mickelson.

Most Aces on the Same Hole in a US Open, **Four**, in the 1989 championship at the Oak Hill CC's 6th hole, in Rochester, New York. The hole was playing at 159 yards. The acers were Doug Weaver, Jerry Pate, Mark Wiebe, and Nick Price. The odds on making that many aces on a hole in one day were pegged at 8.7 million to 1. But that figure did not take into account that the hole was cut in the center of a circular depression in the green, thereby creating a kind of funnel for balls that tippled over the edge and into the "bowl." No one at the USGA ever explained why its otherwise very strict course set-up program allowed such a hole placement.

Highest Seventy-two-Hole Winning Total Score in the US Open (from 1985 through 1941), 331, by Willie Anderson at the Myopia Hunt Club, which was now an eighteen-hole layout. He had rounds of 84–83–83–81.

Highest Winning Total in the US Open (from 1946 to Present— the Open Was Cancelled from 1942 through 1945 due to World War II), 293, in 1963, by Julius Boros, Jackie Cupit, and Arnold Palmer, again at The Country Club, Brookline, Massachusetts. Boros won the playoff with a 70 to Cupit's 73 and Palmer's 76.

Most Consecutive Birdies, **Six**, George Burns, on holes two through seven at Pebble Beach GL, in 1982; Andy Dillard, on holes one through six at Pebble Beach, in 1992.

Most Consecutive Threes, **Eight**, by Hubert Green, on holes nine through sixteen at Baltusrol GC, Springfield, New Jersey, in 1980.

Most Consecutive Opens Started, **Forty-four**, Jack Nicklaus.

Most US Opens Completed, **Thirty-five**, Jack Nicklaus.

Most Top-Five Finishes in the US Open, **Eleven**, Willie Anderson and Jack Nicklaus.

Most Top-Ten Finishes in the US Open, **Eighteen**, Jack Nicklaus.

Longest Par-3 in US Open History (to Date), **288-yard 8th**, at Oakmont CC, 2007.

Longest Par-4 in US Open History (to Date), **525-yard 7th**, at Bethpage Black, 2009.

Longest Par-5 in US Open History (to Date), **667-yard 12th**, at Oakmont CC, 2007.

Most Often Used Site for the US Open, Oakmont CC, with eight (1927, 1935, 1953, 1962, 1973, 1983, 1994, 2007).

Most Astounding, Dramatic, Heroic Comeback in US Open (Indeed, in Sports) History, Ben Hogan, in winning the 1950 championship. In late 1948 Hogan was severely injured when the car he was driving had a head-on highway collision with a Greyhound bus. It was felt by most people that should he survive, which was in doubt at first, he would never play golf again. Only eighteen months later he proved everyone wrong.

After some eight months of intensive physical rehabilitation, during which time he allegedly never swung a golf club (he did in fact hit some chips and putts), Hogan began to practice and play a few rounds. To everyone's great surprise, in January 1950 he entered the Los Angeles Open, and to even greater astonishment he tied for the victory with Sam Snead. Snead would win the playoff, but it was clear that Hogan, who had won the 1948 US Open and established himself once and for all as one of the best players in the game, was back. He entered the 1950 US Open, played at Merion GC, outside Philadelphia, and although playing on legs that would never again regain full strength, he came to the 72nd hole needing a par-4 to tie George Fazio and Lloyd Mangrum for the title. It was his 36th hole of the day (it was when the final two rounds of the Open were played in one day), and although dog-tired he was able to hit a 1-iron (or perhaps a 2-iron) onto the green. This shot, alone, might be considered *The Most Dramatic Single Shot Ever Played in US Open History.* He two-putted to get into a playoff, which he won with a one-under-par 69 to Mangrum's 73 and Fazio's 75.

Most Unpopular Suspension of Amateur Status, Francis Ouimet. Stripped in 1916 on grounds that he had or was planning to open a retail sporting goods store in downtown Boston. USGA president, Frank Woodward, claimed Ouimet was using his celebrity as a champion golfer for financial gain. Ouimet, who became an American folk hero when in 1913 he defeated Harry Vardon and Ted Ray in a playoff for the US Open, was much adored not only for that achievement but also because of his gentlemanly manner and firm belief in amateurism. From a modest economic background, he never did turn to professional golf, although he would certainly have done well on an exhibition circuit following his sensational victory in 1913.

Woodward's edict received considerable, often quite angry, criticism from the general golfing public and almost all the top amateur golfers. It was damned as an "outrage" and a "disintegrating force in golf" and as an example of the USGA's image as a stiff and insensitive ruling body. In 1918, under a new president, and after Ouimet joined the military with the US entry into World War I, the USGA reinstated Ouimet's amateur status. He would go on to win his second US Amateur championship in 1931 (his first came in 1914), play on eight US Walker Cup teams and captain the next four, and was the first American to be "played in" as the Captain of the Royal & Ancient Society of St. Andrews Golfers—a great honor. He would also serve on various USGA committees over the next forty-plus years.

▷ LEASTS

Fewest Eyes Used to Win The US Open, One. Tommy Armour, the famed "Silver Scot," was the victim of a mustard gas explosion while in combat in World War I, and he lost his sight. For his other injuries surgeons inserted metal plates in his head and left arm. During convalescence he regained the sight in his right eye and retained it for the rest of his life. After a brief but accomplished amateur career, the native of Scotland moved to the United States and helped pioneer the PGA Tour. In all, Armour won twenty-four tournaments as a professional, including the US Open (1927), the PGA Championship (1930), and the British Open (1931). All with one eye.

After retiring from competition in 1935, Armour became one of the most sought-after golf teachers in the game, and he had considerable input in the design of the fine clubs produced by the MacGregor Golf Company from the 1930s into the 1960s.

His nephew, Tommy Armour III, was a two-time winner on the PGA Tour and currently plays on the Senior PGA Tour.

Lowest First Thirty-six-Hole Total by the Winner of a US Open, **131** (65–66) by Rory McIlroy, 2011.

Lowest Fifty-four-Hole Total by the Winner of a US Open, **199**, Rory McIlroy, 2011.

Lowest Winning Score in a US Open, **268**, Rory McIlroy, (–16), 2011.

Lowest Last Fifty-four-Hole Total by a Nonwinner of a US Open, **203**, Loren Roberts, 69–64–70, 1994.

Lowest First Thirty-six-Hole Total by a Nonwinner of a US Open, **132**, Ricky Barnes, 67–65, 2009.

Lowest Nine-Hole Score in the US Open, **29**, Neal Lancaster, 1995 and 1996; Vijay Singh, 2003.

Smallest Winner of the US Open, **Freddie McLeod**, who weighed 108 pounds when he won the 1908 title.

Shortest Last Name of a US Open Winner, **Ted Ray** (1930), **Ernie Els** (1994, 1997).

Least Fairway Bunkered US Open Course, **Olympic GC,** with only three; on the 6th hole 245 yards from the tee, and two about fifty yards short of the first green.

Lowest Total Score by an Amateur in US Open, **282** (-2), Jack Nicklaus. 1960. (Runner-up)

Lowest Single-Round Score by an Amateur in the US Open, **65,** James McHale (-6), 1947; Jim Simons (-5) 1971; and Nick Taylor (-5) 2009.

Lowest Single-Round Score in a US Open, **63,** by Johnny Miller (-8) 1973; Jack Nicklaus (-7) 1980; Tom Weiskopf (-7) 1980; V. J. Singh (-7) 2003.

Lowest Total Score by Nonwinner of US Open, **274** (-6), Isao Aoki, 1980; Payne Stewart, 1993.

Youngest Competitor in the US Open, **Tad Fujikawa,** 15 years, 5 months, 7 days, 2006.

Shortest Course for a US Open (since World War II), **Merion GC East,** 6, 528 yds.

Darkest Dark-Horse Winner of the US Open, **Jack Fleck,** 1955, or **Francis Ouimet,** 1913. (See **Biggest or Most Astounding Upset,** above), or **Sam Parks,** 1935, **Tony Manero,** 1936, or **Orville Moody,** 1969.

Lowest US Open Qualifying Round Score, **58,** by Shigeki Maruyama, of Japan. He was 13–under par on the 6,539-yard Woodmont CC South course, in Rockville, Maryland. In the second round, played the same day, Maruyama shot a 74 (+2) on Woodmont's North course. He qualified for the championship, at Pebble Beach, but did not make the cut.

2 the masters

▶ FIRSTS

First Winner of the Masters, **Horton Smith**, 1934. He won it again, in 1936, to become the *First Two-Time Winner of the Tournament.*

First Winner of the Masters in a Playoff, **Gene Sarazen**, 1935. He gained the playoff with one of the most sensational shots in golf history, holing out a 4-wood second shot for a double-eagle on the par-5 15th hole in the final regulation round to pick up three strokes on Craig Wood, the leader in the clubhouse. Sarazen then parred in, and in a thirty-six-hole playoff the next day he defeated Wood, 144–149.

Double-eagles are generally called an "albatross," being a very big bird, but Sarazen called his a "dodo," which is now an extinct bird that was considered dumb, or at least not as smart as an owl, let's say. Sarazen used this term for his feat because he always thought, and quite rightfully, that holing out from 235 yards was largely a matter of dumb luck. However, he did hit a good shot to put luck into the equation. As Branch Rickey put it, "Luck is the residue of design." After all, Sarazen was trying to hole out and was within possible distance.

First Winner of the Masters in First Try, **Gene Sarazen**, 1935. Ironically, or oddly, and no doubt to the surprise of some if not most golf history buffs as a player who would come to define the Masters tournament after his double-eagle in 1935, Sarazen did not play in the 1934 inaugural. He was one of the foremost players in the game at the time, and he said he had some lucrative exhibitions scheduled at the same time. He also had seen the course and didn't think much of it.

The First to Fire Shots in the Masters, **Ralph Stonehouse and John Kinder** were the first golfers to play away in the inaugural Masters, on March 22, 1934.

First Low Amateur (Sort of) in the Masters, **Bobby Jones**, 1934. Jones, of course, was cofounder, with Clifford Roberts, of the tournament and codesigner of the course. He retired from competitive golf in 1930, but almost immediately afterward he began to make a great deal of money from books on golf instruction and on instructional films and from the sale of Bobby Jones Signature Spalding golf clubs. All of which made him, in fact, a professional. He himself would acknowledge that when, some years later, he applied for reinstatement of his amateur status. That he played in the Masters as an amateur was characteristic of the Masters, which, as Tommy Bolt once put it sarcastically, "They make their own rules." Jones was not particularly anxious to play in the 1934 event, or in subsequent ones, but he was prompted by Roberts to do so to help stimulate interest in the event. In all, Jones played in the first twelve Masters (through 1948). He was low amateur twice more (1938, 1942), but he never did better than a tie for 13th overall, his finish in 1934. His best single round was a 72. He finally stopped playing as the illness that would finally cripple him began to worsen.

First Back-to-Back Winner of the Masters, Jack Nicklaus, 1965, 1966. Notable Others: Nick Faldo (1989, 1990), Tiger Woods (2001, 2002).

First Amateur to Finish in Top-Five in the Masters, Frank Stranahan, T2, 1947.

First African American to Play in the Masters, Lee Elder, 1975. For close to a decade the Masters was criticized for having never invited an African American to compete in the event. Finally, in 1974 the tournament's committee altered its rules to say that anyone who wins an official PGA Tour tournament between the end of one Masters and the beginning of the next one is automatically invited. When Lee Elder won the 1974 Monsanto Open a sore point was healed.

First Wire-to-Wire Winner, Craig Wood, 1941. Notable Others: Arnold Palmer (1960), Jack Nicklaus (1972), Raymond Floyd (1976).

First Green Jacket Awarded to the Winner, 1949, to Sam Snead, who came up with the idea. Members of Augusta National had been wearing green jackets at the tournament since 1937.

First Britons to Play in the Masters, Harry Cooper, C. G. Stevens, and C. T. Wilson, 1934. Stevens and Wilson were amateurs. Cooper and Stevens withdrew after three and two rounds respectively; Wilson finished 59th. Cooper was born in England but came to the United States as a young boy and essentially made his career in America. While he didn't play well in this Masters, Cooper became one of the best players in American golf through the 1930s and was twice a runner-up in the Masters.

First Asians (and Japanese) to Play in the Masters, Torchy Toda, Chick Chin, 1936. Toda tied for 29th, Chin tied for 20th.

First Canadian to Play in the Masters, C. Ross Somerville, an amateur, in 1934.

First Argentineans to Play in the Masters, **Enrique Bertolino, Martin Pose**, both in 1940. Pose finished 37th, Bertolino 50th.

First South African to Play in the Masters, **Bobby Locke**, 1947, 14th.

First Brazilian to Play in the Masters, **Ricardo Rossi**, 1953, T55th.

First Frenchman to Play in the Masters, **Albert Pelisser**, 1952 (wd).

First New Zealander to Play in the Masters, **Bob Charles** (Amateur), 1958 (mc).

First Belgian to Play in the Masters, **Flory Van Donck**, 1958, T32nd.

First Spaniard to Play in the Masters, **Angel Miguel**, 1959, T25th.

First Colombian to Play in the Masters, **Miguel Sala**, 1961, 38th.

First Mexican to Play in the Masters, **Antonio Cerda**, 1961, T24th.

First Scotsman to Play in the Masters, **David Blair** (Amateur), 1962 (mc).

First German to Play in the Masters, **Bernhard Langer**, 1982 (mc).

First Australian to Play in the Masters, **Jim Ferrier**, 1940 (26th).

First Philippine to Play in the Masters, **Ben Arda**, 1962 (mc).

First Hollander to Play in the Masters, **Gerry DeWitt**, 1963 (mc).

First Taiwan Chinese to Play in the Masters, **Cheng Ching-Po**, 1963 (T15th).

First Irishman to Play in the Masters, Joe Carr (Amateur), 1967 (55th).

First Peruvian to Play in the Masters, Raul Travieso, 1968 (mc).

First Thai to Play in the Masters, Sukree Onsham, 1970 (mc).

First Italian to Play in the Masters, Roberto Bernardini, 1970 (mc).

First Mainland Chinese to Play in the Masters, Lu Liang-Huan, 1969 (mc).

First South Korean to Play in the Masters, Hahn Chang Sang, 1973 (mc).

First Welshman to Play in the Masters, Duncan Evans (Amateur), 1981 (mc).

First Zimbabwean to Play in the Masters, Nick Price, 1984 (mc).

First Swede to Play in the Masters, Christian Hardin (Amateur), 1989 (mc).

First Fijian to Play in the Masters, Vijay Singh, 1997 (T17th).

First Dane to Play in the Masters, Thomas Bjorn, 1999 (mc).

First Namibian to Play in the Masters, Trevor Dodds, 1999 (mc).

First International Golfer to Win the Masters, Gary Player, South Africa (1961).

First Continental European to Win the Masters, Seve Ballesteros, 1980.

First Three-Time Winner of the Masters, Jimmy Demaret, 1940, 1947, 1950.

First Four-Time Winner of the Masters, Arnold Palmer, 1958, 1960, 1962, 1964.

First Five- and Six-Time Winner of the Masters, Jack Nicklaus, 1963, 1965, 1966, 1972, 1975, 1986. The last one was the best. Jack, at age 46, shot a brilliant 65 in the final round that included a run of eagle, birdie, and birdie from the 15th through the 17th holes. He won by a shot over Tom Kite.

FIRST WINNERS OF THE MASTERS, BY STATE BORN IN

First from California, **George Archer,** 1969. Notable Others: Billy Casper (1970), Craig Stadler (1982), Tiger Woods (1997, 2001, 2002, 2005), Phil Mickelson (2004, 2006, 2010).

First from Connecticut, **Doug Ford,** 1957.

First from Georgia, **Claude Harmon,** 1948. Notable Others: Tommy Aaron (1973), Larry Mize (1987).

First from Illinois, **Bob Goalby,** 1968.

First from Indiana, **Frank Urban "Fuzzy" Zoeller,** 1979.

First from Iowa, **Zach Johnson,** 2007.

First from Massachusetts, **Henry Picard,** 1938.

First from Missouri, **Horton Smith,** 1934. Notable Other: Tom Watson (1991).

First from New York, **Gene Sarazen,** 1935. Notable Other: Craig Wood (1941).

First from North Carolina, **Raymond Floyd,** 1976. Notable Other: Mark O'Meara (1998).

First from Ohio, **Herman Keiser,** 1946. Notable Others: Gay Brewer (1967), Jack Nicklaus (1963, 1965, 1966, 1972, 1975, 1986).

First from Pennsylvania, **Arnold Palmer,** 1958. Notable Other: Art Wall (1959).

First from Tennessee, **Cary Middlecoff,** 1955.

First from Texas, **Byron Nelson**, 1937. Notable Others: Ralph Guldahl (1939), Jimmy Demaret (1940, 1947, 1950), Ben Hogan (1951, 1953), Jack Burke Jr. (1956), Charles Coody (1971), Ben Crenshaw (1984, 1995).

First from Virginia, **Sam Snead**, 1949.

First from Washington, **Fred Couples**, 1992.

FIRST INTERNATIONAL WINNERS OF THE MASTERS, BY NATIVE COUNTRY

First South African, **Gary Player**, 1961. Notable Others: Trevor Immelman (2008), Charl Schwartzl (2011).

First Spaniard, **Seve Ballesteros**, 1980. Notable Other: Jose Maria Olazabal (1999).

First German, **Bernhard Langer**, 1985.

First Scotsman, **Sandy Lyle**, 1988.

First Englishman, **Nick Faldo**, 1989.

First Welshman, **Ian Woosnam**, 1991.

First Fijian, **V. J. Singh**, 2000.

First Argentinean, **Angel Cabrera**, 2009.

First Canadian, **Mike Weir**, 2003.*

*Weir is also *The First Left-Handed Golfer to Win the Masters.*

First Left-Hander to Play in the Masters, **Gene Ferrell**, 1956. He DQ'd.

First to Make a Hole-in-One, **Ross Somerville**, 1934, at the 16th, then a 145 yarder. He hit a mashie niblick (8-iron).

First to Break Par in All Four Rounds, **Jimmy Demaret**, in 1947, when he won for the second time, with rounds of 69–71–70–71.

First Cut Instituted, **1957**, to top forty and ties. Some of the stars who missed included Ben Hogan, Cary Middlecoff, Gene Littler, Bob Rosburg, and Mike Souchak.

First Use of "Amen Corner" to Identify the Conjunction of the 11th Green, 12th Hole, and 13th Tee, **1958.** The author of the term was Herbert Warren Wind, the doyen of American golf writers. He took it from an old jazz song entitled "Shouting at Amen Corner." Wind was inspired by the events at Amen Corner in the 1958 Masters, when Arnold Palmer got a favorable ruling on the par-3 12th hole. His tee shot plugged in rain-soaked turf behind the green. It was first ruled, by the referee on site, that there was no embedded ball rule in play and that Palmer had to play the ball as it lay. Palmer argued that it was an incorrect judgment and that he would play the plugged ball, and then play another from a dropped (and much better) lie in lieu of a recall of the ruling. He made a five with the embedded ball, a three with the dropped ball. Palmer then holed an eighteen-foot putt for an eagle three on the 13th hole, and two holes later the tournament chairmen, Cliff Roberts and Bobby Jones, overruled the 12th hole onsite referee, Arthur Lacey, and Palmer was given a three on that hole. It led to his first Masters victory.

First Sudden-Death Playoff, **1979.** Frank Urban "Fuzzy" Zoeller won on the second playoff hole (the 11th on the course) with a birdie 3. He defeated Ed Sneed and Tom Watson. The system was instituted in 1976.

▶ MOSTS

Tallest Winner, **George Archer,** 6'5", 1969.

Biggest Fifty-four-Hole Lead Lost, **Six,** in the 1966 Masters, Greg Norman, who had been in numerous close struggles to win the tournament, frittered away the lead to Nick Faldo, with whom he was paired in the final round. Norman had a 78 to Faldo's superb 67, which gave Faldo the victory by five strokes. An argument can be made that Norman didn't lose so much as Faldo won, but given Norman's overall success as a player and the unusually high score he shot, that he lost is closer to the truth.

Oldest Winner of the Masters, **Jack Nicklaus**, 46 years, 2 months, 23 days, 1986.

Most Victories in Masters, **Six**, Jack Nicklaus, 1963, 1965, 1966, 1972, 1975, 1986.

Most Runner-up Finishes, **Four**, Ben Hogan, Jack Nicklaus, Tom Weiskopf.

Oldest Runner-up, **Raymond Floyd**, 49 years, 4 months, 8 days.

Heaviest Winner, **Craig Stadler**, 235 pounds.

Biggest Comeback Round, **Craig Wood**, in 1936, he went 88–67. He then shot 69, 76 to tie for 20th.

Biggest Regress Round, **Mike Donald**, in 1990 went 64–82. He then shot 77–76 to finish 47th.

State with Most Masters Victories, **Texas**, twelve, Jack Burke Jr. (one), Charles Coody (one), Ben Crenshaw (two), Jimmy Demaret (three), Ralph Guldahl (one), Ben Hogan (two), Byron Nelson (two).

Most Consecutive Cuts Made in the Masters, **Twenty-three**, Gary Player, 1959–1982.

Most Consecutive Top-Ten Finishes, **Fourteen**, Ben Hogan, 1939–1956.

Most Cuts Made (Career), **Thirty-seven**, Jack Nicklaus.

Most Birdies (Career), **506**, Jack Nicklaus.

Most Birdies in One Round, **Eleven**, Anthony Kim, 2009 Masters.

Most Consecutive Birdies in One Round, **Seven**, Steve Pate, 1999 (from 7th hole).

Most Eagles (Career), **Twenty-four**, Jack Nicklaus (three on par-4s, twenty-one on par-5s).

Most Sub-Par Rounds (Career), **Seventy-one**, out of 163 played, Jack Nicklaus.

Most Consecutive Sub-Par Rounds, **Ten**, Tiger Woods, 2000, 2001, 2002.

Most Eagles in One Tournament by an Individual, **Four**, Bruce Crampton, 1974.

Highest Winning Score, **289**, Sam Snead (1954), Jack Burke Jr., 1956.

Most Sudden-Death Playoff Victories, **Two**, Nick Faldo, 1989–1990.

Longest Stretch of Holes without a Bogey, **Fifty**, Geoff Ogilvy, 2007.

Widest Margin of Victory, **Twelve strokes**, Tiger Woods, 1997.

Oldest to Finish in Top Five, **Jimmy Demaret**, in 1962, when he was 51 years, 10 months, 28 days. He tied for 5th.

Oldest to Finish in Top Ten, **Jack Nicklaus**, in 1998, when he was 58 years, 2 months, 21 days. He tied for 6th.

Most Emotional Victory, **1995**, when Ben Crenshaw won his second Masters a week after his lifelong mentor, Harvey Penick, passed away. Crenshaw went into a deep sob after holing the final putt.

Most Frequent Winner in a Playoff, **Nick Faldo**, two, 1989 and 1990.

Most Frequent Loser in a Playoff, **Ben Hogan**, two, 1942, 1954.

▶ LEASTS

Youngest Winner of the Masters, **Tiger Woods,** in 1997, when he was 21 years, 3 months, 14 days.

Shortest Winner of the Masters, **Ian Woosnam,** in 1991, at 5'4½" 1991.

Shortest Surname Winner, **Four letters,** Art Wall, Doug Ford, Larry Mize, Sandy Lyle, Mike Weir.

Lowest Single Round, **63,** Nick Price, 1986; Greg Norman, 1996.

Lowest Front Nine Score, **30,** Johnny Miller, 1975, Greg Norman, 1988, K. J. Choi, 2004.

Lowest Back Nine Score, **29,** Mark Calcavecchia, 1992; David Toms, 1998.

Lowest Nine-Hole Score by a Senior (50+), **30,** by Ben Hogan, on the back nine in 1967, when he was 54 years old. He shot 66 on the day, shot 77 the next day, and finished tied for 10th.

Lowest Seventy-two Hole by a Senior, **283 (–5),** Jack Nicklaus, at 58, 1998.

Lowest Winning Score, **270,** Tiger Woods, 1997 (70–66–65–69).

Youngest Top-Ten Finisher, **Jack Nicklaus,** 21 years, 2 months, 20 days, 1961. He tied for 7th.

Least Likely (Darkest Dark-Horse) Winner of the Masters, **Herman Keiser,** 1946.

Lowest Low-Amateur Total Score, **281 (–7),** Charles Coe Jr., 1961.

Youngest To Make Cut, **Matteo Manassero,** was 16 years, 11 months, 22 days old when he shot 71–76 in the 2010 tournament. He finished with 73–72 to tie for 36th.

3 **the pga championship**

▶ FIRSTS: MATCH PLAY

Match play was the format used until 1958.

First Winner of the PGA Championship, **Jim Barnes**, 1916. He was born in England.

First American-born Winner of the PGA Championship, **Walter Hagen**, 1921. In the day, American golfers were referred to as "homebreds," a reference to the fact that the competition in the American game up to the start of Hagen's emergence had been dominated by golfers who emigrated from Great Britain.

First Medalist to Win the Championship, **Walter Hagen**, 1926, 140 (−4), at the Salisbury Golf Links, Westbury, Long Island, New York.

First Winner in Overtime, **Gene Sarazen**, who defeated Walter Hagen on the 38th hole, 1923, at the Pelham CC, Pelham, New York.

Most PGA Championship Victories, **Five**, Walter Hagen, in 1921, 1924, 1925, 1926, 1927. Hagen qualifying for Most Consecutive Victories in the PGA embellishes this record.

Hagen didn't defend his title in 1922, opting instead to play a lucrative exhibition schedule. And when Leo Diegel broke Hagen's streak in 1928, he did not immediately receive the trophy. The irrepressible Hagen had it in his possession for three years and didn't know where it was when it was time to give it up. It was found among his other belongings in the factory where his clubs were made.

▶ FIRSTS: STROKE PLAY

First Winner of the PGA Championship, **Dow Finsterwald,** 1958, with a score of 276, 4–under par at the Llanerch CC, Haverton, Pennsylvania. The championship went to stroke play in large part because of television demands. For one thing, the networks were not keen about the potential of having two lesser-known golfers in the final match. And for another, television technology at the time did not allow for covering more than three or four holes, which were invariably the last ones on the course. What if a semifinal or final ended before they reached camera range?

First Wire-to-Wire Winner, **Bobby Nichols,** 1964, at Columbus CC, Columbus, Ohio, with rounds of 64–71–69–77. He won by three over Jack Nicklaus and Arnold Palmer.

First Winner in Eighteen-Hole Playoff, **Jerry Barber,** over Don January, 67–68, 1961, at Olympia Fields CC, outside Chicago. January led Barber by four shots with three regulation holes to play. Barber then holed a birdie putt of twenty feet, a par putt of forty feet, and a sixty footer for a birdie to tie January at 277. Barber won the eighteen-hole playoff by a stroke with more outstanding long putting.

First Sudden-Death Playoff Winner, **Lanny Wadkins,** over Gene Littler on the third extra hole, 1977, at Pebble Beach.

First to Score All Four Rounds in the 60s, **Arnold Palmer**, 1964. But he didn't win. Bobby Nichols won by four strokes over Palmer and Jack Nicklaus.

↙ FIRST WINNERS OF THE PGA CHAMPIONSHIP, BY STATE BORN IN

First from Alabama, **Larry Nelson**, 1981.

First from Arizona, **Rich Beem**, 2002.

First from Arkansas, **Paul Runyan**, 1934. Notable Other: John Daly (1991).

First from California, **Olin Dutra**, 1932. Notable Others: Bob Rosburg (1959), Al Geiberger (1966), Dave Stockton (1970, 1976), Tiger Woods (1999, 2000, 2006, 2007), Phil Mickelson (2005).

First from Connecticut, **Doug Ford**, 1955. Notable Other: Julius Boros (1968).

First from Florida, **Paul Azinger**, 1993. Notable Other: Shaun Micheel (2003).

First from Illinois, **Jerry Barber**, 1961.

First from Indiana, **Bob Hamilton**, 1944.

First from Louisiana, **Lionel Hebert**, 1957. Notable Others: Jay Hebert (1960), David Toms (2001).

First from Massachusetts, **Henry Picard**, 1939.

First from Michigan, **Leo Diegel**, 1928. Notable Other: Walter Burkemo (1953).

First from Missouri, **Johnny Revolta**, 1935. Notable Other: Payne Stewart (1989).

First from New Jersey, **Vic Ghezzi**, 1941.

First from New York, **Walter Hagen,** 1921. Notable Others: Gene Sarazen (1922, 1923, 1933), Tom Creavy (1931), Jim Turnesa (1952), Jeff Sluman (1988).

First from North Carolina, **Raymond Floyd,** 1969. Notable Other: Davis Love III (1997).

First from Ohio, **Denny Shute,** 1936. Notable Others: Chick Harbert (1954), Jack Nicklaus (1963, 1971, 1973, 1975, 1980).

First from Oklahoma, **Bob Tway,** 1986.

First from Texas, **Byron Nelson,** 1940, 1945. Notable Others: Ben Hogan (1946, 1948), Jack Burke Jr. (1956), Dave Marr (1965), Don January (1967), Lee Trevino (1974, 1984), John Mahaffey (1978), Mark Brooks (1996).

First from Virginia, **Sam Snead,** 1942. Notable Others: Chandler Harper (1950), Lanny Wadkins (1977).

First from Vermont, **Keegan Bradley,** 2011.

FIRST NATIVE-COUNTRY INTERNATIONAL WINNERS OF THE PGA CHAMPIONSHIP

First Englishman, **Jim Barnes,** 1916.

First Scotsman, **Jock Hutchison,** 1920.

First Australian, **Jim Ferrier,** 1947. Notable Others: David Graham (1979), Wayne Grady (1990), Steve Elkington (1995).

First South African, **Gary Player,** 1962. Notable Other: Nick Price (1992).

First Fijian, **V. J. Singh,** 1998.

First South Korean, **Y. E. Yang,** 2009.

First Irishman, **Padraig Harrington,** 2008.

First German, **Martin Kaymer,** 2010.

First PGA of America Senior Champion, **Jock Hutchison,** 1937.

First PGA of America Club Professional National Championship, **1968,** won by Howell Fraser, Mountain Ridge CC, West Caldwell, New Jersey.

▶ MOSTS: MATCH PLAY

Largest Margin of Victory in Final, **8 & 7,** Paul Runyan over Sam Snead in 1938 championship, at Shawnee-on-the-Delaware, Pennsylvania. The pint-sized Runyan was outhit off the tee by up to one hundred yards, but he outplayed Snead around the greens. Runyan was a genius at the short game and would pass that legacy down through the years and have a positive impact on Jack Nicklaus's game. Nicklaus would get short-game help from Phil Rodgers, who was a Runyan disciple.

Most Finals Reached, **Six,** Walter Hagen, 1921, 1923, 1924, 1925, 1926, 1927. He won all but in 1923.

Most Semifinals, **Eight,** Walter Hagen, 1916, 1921, 1923, 1924, 1925, 1926, 1927, 1929.

Most Consecutive Times in Finals, **Five,** Walter Hagen.

Most Consecutive Matches Won, **Twenty-two,** Walter Hagen.

Most Years Qualified for Match Play, **Twenty-eight,** Gene Sarazen.

Most Matches Played, **Eighty-two,** Gene Sarazen.

Most Matches Won, **Fifty-seven,** Gene Sarazen.

Most Holes Played, 2,221, Gene Sarazen.

Highest-Winning Percentage of Matches Played, 82 percent, Byron Nelson (thirty-seven wins, eight losses) and Walter Burkemo (twenty-seven wins, six losses).

Most Runners-Up in PGA (Either Format), Three, Byron Nelson.

▶ MOSTS: STROKE PLAY

Most Cuts Made, Twenty-seven, Jack Nicklaus and Raymond Floyd.

Most Top-Three Finishes, Jack Nicklaus.

Most Top-Five Finishes, Jack Nicklaus.

Most Top-Ten Finishes, Jack Nicklaus.

Most Runners-Up in PGA, Four, Jack Nicklaus.

Biggest Winning Margin, Seven strokes, Jack Nicklaus, 1980. On rounds of 70–69–66–69–274 over the formidable Oak Hill CC course, Rochester, New York.

Highest First-Round Score by Winner, 75 (+4), John Mahaffey, 1978.

Highest Winning Score, 287 (–1), Larry Nelson and Lanny Wadkins, 1987, at PGA National GC, Palm Beach Gardens, Florida. Nelson won the playoff. The high score is attributable in some part to the event being played in August in Florida, when the heat and humidity was life threatening. Nelson won on the first extra hole, with a par-4.

Oldest Winner, Julius Boros, 48 years, 4 months, 18 days when he won in 1968 at the Pecan Valley CC, San Antonio, Texas.

Winner with Longest Surname, Finsterwald, Dow, in 1958.

Biggest Comeback to Win the PGA, **Seven strokes,** by John Mahaffey, 1978. With a final-round 66 (–5) at the Oakmont CC, Oakmont, Pennsylvania, he caught Tom Watson and Jerry Pate, then took the title with a twelve-foot birdie putt on the second extra hole.

Most Appearances in PGA Championship, **Thirty-seven,** Jack Nicklaus and Arnold Palmer.

Most Rounds Played in PGA Championship, **128,** Jack Nicklaus.

▶ LEASTS: MATCH PLAY

Smallest Winner, **Paul Runyan,** 5'3", 120 pounds. Runyan won the championship twice, in 1934 and 1938.

Youngest Winner, **Gene Sarazen,** at 20 years, 5 months, 22 days, in 1922 at the Oakmont CC, Oakmont, Pennsylvania.

Lowest Thirty-six-Hole Qualifying Score, **134,** Jim Ferrier, 1946 (winner); Stewart "Skip" Alexander, 1948; Johnny Palmer, 1953.

Fewest Total Number of Holes Played by a Winner, **154,** Leo Diegel, 1928 and 1929; Gene Sarazen, 1933; Ben Hogan, 1946.

Lowest First Prize, **$500,** 1916–1930.

▶ LEASTS: STROKE PLAY

Lowest Winning Total Score, **265** (–15), David Toms, 2001, at the Atlanta Athletic Club, Duluth, Georgia. At that, he won by only one stroke, over Phil Mickelson.

Lowest Winning Total Score to Par, **270** (–18), Tiger Woods, Bob May. At the 2000 championship at the Valhalla GC, Louisville, Kentucky. May, a midlevel Tour player, had a career week. After a first-round 72 (E), he fired three straight 66s to gain a playoff with the hottest player in the game. Woods won the playoff. (See next entry.) Woods again shot 270 to win outright the 2006 championship, this time on a par-72 course, Medinah CC, outside Chicago.

The First PGA Championship with a Three-Hole Aggregate-Score Playoff, **2000** when Tiger Woods defeated Bob May by one stroke with a birdie and two pars.

Youngest Winner, **Tiger Woods**, 23 years, 7 months, in 1999, at Medinah CC.

Lowest Scoring Average Seventy-five Rounds or More, **71.37**, Jack Nicklaus, 128 rounds.

Lowest Scoring Average, Fifty Rounds or More, **70.71**, Phil Mickelson, sixty-two rounds.

Lowest Scoring Average, Twenty-five Rounds or More, **69.73**, Tiger Woods, forty-four rounds.

Lowest Score by Nonwinner, **266** (**-14**), Phil Mickelson, 2001, at The Atlanta Athletic Club, Duluth, Georgia. David Toms won with 265.

Lowest One-Round Score, **63** (**-7**), Bruce Crampton, 1975; Raymond Floyd (-7), 1982; Gary Player (-9), 1984; Vijay Singh (-8), 1993; Michael Bradley (-8), 1993; Brad Faxon (-8), 1995; Jose Maria Olazabal (-9), 2000; Mark O'Meara (-7) 2001; Thomas Bjorn (-7), 2005; Tiger Woods (-7), 2007.

Shortest Last Name Winner(s), Olin **Dutra** (1932); Doug **Ford** (1955); Dave **Marr** (1965); Bob **Tway** (1986); John **Daly** (1991); Davis **Love III** (the numerals don't count), 1997. David **Toms** (2001).

Least Likely (or Darkest Dark-Horse) Winners, **Tom Creavy**, 1931; **Bob Hamilton**, 1944; **John Daly**, 1991. Daly, a ninth alternate qualifier, famously got into the tournament when Nick Price had to withdraw and three alternates ahead of him declined to fill the vacancy. Daly drove overnight from his home in Arkansas to the Crooked Stick GC, Carmel, Indiana, had an opening round 69, then rounds of 67–69–71 (–2) to win by two strokes over Bruce Lietzke. The victory propelled the hitherto unknown Daly, an exceptionally long hitter, into the game's limelight.

4 the ryder cup

▷ FIRSTS

First Ryder Cup Match, **1927.** (The Matches are held every two years.) First players to represent the US were: Walter Hagen (Captain), Leo Diegel, Al Espinosa, Johnny Farrell, Gene Sarazen, Johnny Golden, Bill Mehlhorn, Joe Turnesa, Al Watrous. Members of first British team: Aubrey Boomer, Archie Compston, George Duncan, George Gadd, Arthur Havers, Herbert Jolly, Ted Ray (Captain), Fred Robson, Charles Whitcombe. The Ryder Cup Matches were generated in large part by the PGA of America as a kind of job action. Until 1920 private golf clubs in the United States were often hiring Scottish and British born head professionals on the premise that having been born and raised where the game of golf originated, they were better schooled in it. The PGA of America believed that if its homebred professionals showed they could compete successfully against Great Britain's pros the members of American clubs would be more inclined to hire them.

First Ryder Cup Winning Team, **United States,** 9½ to 2½, 1927. It was played at the Worcester CC, Worcester, Massachusetts.

First Non-British European Team Captain, **Seve Ballesteros,** 2004.

First Brothers to Compete on the Same Team, **Charles and Ernest Whitcombe,** Great Britain, 1935.

First Brothers-in-Law to Compete on the Same Team, **Jerry Pate and Bruce Lietzke,** United States, 1981.

First Ryder Cup Played on European Continent, **1997,** at Valderrrama GC, Sotogrande, Spain.

First Ryder Cup Played in Ireland, **2006,** at The K Club, Straffan, County Kildare.

First African American to Play on US Ryder Cup Team, **Lee Elder,** 1979.

First Year When American Players Were Paid to Play, **1999.** Each player received $100,000, and the money was distributed to charities of their choice and other good works.

▶ MOSTS

Oldest Ryder Cup Player (American Team), **Raymond Floyd,** 51 years, 20 months, 1993; (European Team), **Ted Ray,** 50 years, 2 months, 5 days, 1927.

Oldest Team Captain (American Team), **Sam Snead,** 57 years, 3 months, 25 days, 1969; (European Team), **J. H. Taylor,** 62 years, 3 months, 7 days, 1933.

Highest Margin of Team Victory, **Fifteen points** (United States, 23½, 8½), 1967.

Most Times a Ryder Cup Player, **Eleven,** Nick Faldo (European Team), **Eight,** Lanny Wadkins, Raymond Floyd, Billy Casper (American Team).

Most Matches Played, **Thirty-seven,** Billy Casper (American Team), **Forty-six,** Nick Faldo (European Team).

Most Singles Matches Won (American Team), **Six,** Arnold Palmer, Billy Casper; (European Team), **Six,** Nick Faldo, Colin Montgomerie.

Most Singles Matches Lost (American Team), **Four,** Raymond Floyd, Phil Mickelson, Jack Nicklaus, Mark O'Meara; (European Team), **Ten,** Christy O'Connor Sr.

Pairings with Most Wins (American Team), **David Toms and Phil Mickelson,** six; (European Team), **Seve Ballesteros and Jose Maria Olazabal,** fifteen.

▶ LEASTS

Youngest US Team Captain (American Team), **Arnold Palmer,** 34, 1963; (European Team), **Charles Whitcombe,** 35 years, 9 months, 5 days, 1931.

Youngest Ryder Cup Players (American Team), **Horton Smith,** 21 years, 4 days, 1929; (European Team), **Sergio Garcia,** 19 years, 8 months, 15 days, 1999.

5 the "british" open and amateur

▶ FIRSTS

First British Open* Championship, **1860**, over thirty-six holes at Prestwick GC, Scotland; won by Willie Park, with a score of 174. It is listed in the record books as an Open but it wasn't really, as only professionals were allowed to enter. However, the next British Open, in 1861, allowed amateur players to enter, and it then became true to its designation. And has been ever since.

*In the UK it is called, rather ego- or perhaps ethnocentrically, simply The Open, which is or was acceptable when it was the only Open in the game. It hasn't been since 1895. However, in deference to the British/Scottish contributions to the Old Game, we will refer to it as The Open.

First Winner at Thirty-six Holes, **Willie Park**. It went to a seventy-two-hole event in 1862.

First Multiple Winner, **Tom Morris Sr.,** four, 1861, 1862, 1864, 1867 (all at thirty-six holes).

First Hole-in-One in The Open, **1868**, by "Young" Tom Morris. He hit an 8-iron on the second hole, Prestwick GC, Scotland. He won the championship.

▶ FIRSTS: "MODERN" ERA 1892 TO THE PRESENT

First Winner at Seventy-two Holes, **Harold Hilton**, 1892, with a score of 305, at Muirfield GC, Scotland.

First Amateur to Win The Open or any other National Open Championship, **Harold Hilton** won The Open a second time, in 1897, at Hoylake with a score of 317; he also became the *First Member of the Host Club to Win The Open*.

First Back-to-Back Winner, **John H. Taylor**, 1894, 1895.

First (and Only) Six-Time Winner, **Harry Vardon**, in 1896, 1898, 1899, 1903, 1911, 1914.

First Immigrant American to Win The Open, **Jock Hutchison**, 1921.

First to Break 70, **J. H. Taylor**, 1904, with a final round of 68; he finished second. In the same event James Braid and Jack White had rounds of 69. They played at the Royal St. George and St. Anne's GC, in England. Jack White won the title.

First Non-Anglo Winner, **Arnaud Massy**, of France, in 1907 at Hoylake, England, with a score of 312. A Frenchman winning this championship stirred or begrudged the hosts to claim that somehow or other his Frenchness must be overlooked. He was referred to in British golfing circles as "A Frenchman with a Scots soul."

First American, and International Winner of the British Amateur, **Walter Travis**, in 1904 at the Royal St. George's GC, England. Born in Australia but immigrated to the United States as a young boy and became an American citizen. Travis was quite short in height and a short hitter of the ball (with a fine swing, however). He made his way as a very accurate ball striker and a master putter, brilliant strategist, and dogged competitor. Travis took up golf late, at 35, which made his success as a competitor all the more remarkable. He had won the US Amateur championship three times, in 1900, 1901, and 1903, and a number of lesser regional and local championships.

Travis, who would come to known as "The Old Man," wore a beard and was aloof and somewhat gruff in manner, which especially put off the British when he played in the 1904 British Amateur. The R&A folks did not take his victory happily. Indeed, although they waited a couple of years so as to not appear resentful, the R&A barred the "Schenectady" putter Travis used so deftly to win its championship. (More on the putter, a **First**, in the section on **Equipment**.) Finally, Travis contributed much more to the game than good play. He was a fine golf architect. Among his works in this area was the Westchester CC, in New York, which for many years was the site of a regular PGA Tour event and was considered the best type of layout to prep for a US Open. Travis also founded *The American Golfer*, the first significant American golf periodical.

First Homebred American to Win the British Amateur, **Jesse Sweetser**, 1926, at Muirfield.

First Homebred American to Win the British Amateur and Open in the Same Year, **Bobby Jones**, in 1930. It was his only victory in the British Amateur and was part of his famous "Grand Slam."

First Amateur Winner of The Open, **Bobby Jones**, 1926. Jones would successfully defend the title, in 1927.

First Scot to Win The Open, **Willie Auchterlonie**, 1893. Notable Others: Sandy Lyle (1985), Paul Lawrie (1999).

First Englishman to Win The Open, **John H. Taylor**, 1894. Notable Others: Harry Vardon (1896, 1898, 1899, 1903, 1911, 1914),

Ted Ray (1912), Henry Cotton (1934, 1937, 1948), Tony Jacklin (1969), Nick Faldo (1987, 1990, 1992).

First Frenchman to Win The Open, **Arnaud Massy** (see above).

First American to Win The Open, **Walter Hagen**, 1922. Hagen would win it three more times, in 1924, 1928, 1929.

First South African to Win The Open, **Bobby Locke**, 1949. Locke would win three more, including a back-to-back in 1950, 1952, and 1957. Notable Others: Gary Player (1959, 1968, 1974), Louis Oosthuizen (2010).

First Australian, **Peter Thomson**, 1954. Notable Others: Kel Nagle (1960), Greg Norman (1986, 1993), Ian Baker-Finch (1991).

First New Zealander, **Bob Charles**, 1963. Charles was also the *First Left-Handed Golfer to Win a Major Championship* when he defeated the American, Phil Rodgers, in a thirty-six-hole playoff at Royal Lytham and St. Annes.

First Argentinean, **Roberto DeVicenzo**, 1967.

First Spaniard, **Seve Ballesteros**, 1979.

First Irishman, **Fred Daly**, 1947. Notable Other: Padraig Harrington (2007, 2008), Darren Clarke (2011). Clarke is from Northern Ireland, but Irish is Irish, don't you know.

First Zimbabwean, **Nick Price**, 1994.

First American Winners: Because Americans have been such prominent contenders in The Open, we here provide first winners by state where born.

First from Alabama, **Stewart Cink**, 2009.

First from Arkansas, **John Daly**, 1995.

First from California, **Tony Lema**, 1964. Notable Others: Tiger Woods (2005, 2006).

First from Florida, **David Duval,** 2001.

First from Georgia, **Bobby Jones,** 1926.

First from Minnesota, **Tom Lehman,** 1996.

First from Missouri, **Tom Watson,** 1975. Watson would win the title five times in all, the others in 1977, 1980, 1982, 1983.

First from Nebraska, **Mark Calcavecchia,** 1989.

First from New York, **Walter Hagen,** 1922. Notable Other: Gene Sarazen (1932).

First from North Carolina, **Mark O'Meara,** 1996. O'Meara actually spent most of his formative years in southern California but was born in North Carolina.

First from Ohio, **Denny Shute,** 1933. Notable Others: Jack Nicklaus (1966, 1970, 1978), Tom Weiskopf (1973).

First from Pennsylvania, **Arnold Palmer,** 1961. Palmer began playing The Open in 1960 (he finished second), and through his popularity he revived a stagnant interest in the championship, at least in the United States, and brought it back to full international stature.

First from Tennessee, **Ben Curtis,** 2003.

First from Texas, **Ben Hogan,** 1953. Notable Others: Lee Trevino (1971, 1972), Bill Rogers (1981), Justin Leonard (1997).

First from Virginia, **Sam Snead,** 1946.

First Winner of The Open Using the Gutta Percha Ball, **Allan Robertson,** 1858. Irony here. Robertson despised the coming of the gutta percha ball, and in fact fired his assistant, the then young Tom Morris, who became "Old Tom," for playing with the new "guttie." It was not so much that Robertson was a hardbound traditionalist. He made a healthy part of his living making the featherie balls that the "guttie" replaced. The featherie, each made by hand, was a bag of leather filled with boiled goose feathers. The price of just one ball was dear, and it didn't hold up very well in poor weather, not to mention from the abrasions of being struck. But when it came to his personal welfare in competition, Robertson had no qualms about using the livelier "guttie."

First Winner of The Open Using the Haskell Ball, **Alexander Herd,** 1902. Other golfers of the time did not immediately jump onto the livelier Haskell bandwagon that appeared around this time. In at least one case it took a lot of convincing that it was the better ball; the great Harry Vardon didn't switch to the Haskell for some ten years, although it was probably because he was contracted for that long to play the gutta percha Vardon Flyer.

First Winner of The Open Using the Larger American Ball, **Gary Player,** 1974, at Royal Lytham and St. Annes. In 1968 the British tour professionals began using the 1.68 inch diameter American ball rather than the 1.62 inch ball that had been used for a half century in the UK and wherever the R&A had jurisdiction. The thinking was, the American ball was harder to play in windy conditions, which were so prevalent in Britain, and by learning to use it they would become better players and more competitive against the Americans. It worked, almost immediately. In 1968 Tony Jacklin, a very talented young British pro who won the 1969 British Open, played on the US PGA Tour and won one tournament and had high finishes in a number of others. Then, in 1970 at the Hazeltine CC, in Minneapolis, Minnesota, Jacklin became the first Briton to win the US Open in fifty years, a victory that was sparked by a first round 70 in winds that gusted up to forty mph. That same day Arnold Palmer, Gary Player, and Jack Nicklaus shot rounds of 79, 80, and 81, respectively. For all that, the R&A did not make the larger ball mandatory in The Open until 1974, when Gary Player won the title for the second time.

First to Score a Hat Trick in The Open (Win Three in a Row), **Peter Thomson.** Thomson won five Opens in all (1954, 1955, 1956, 1958, 1965), and all of them playing the smaller British ball. Ever since the larger American ball became the standard he has strongly advocated a return to the smaller one. Of course.

First Back-to-Back Winner of The Open (at Seventy-two Holes), **John H. Taylor,** 1894, 1895.

First British Amateur Championship, **1885.** Won by A. F. Mac-Fie, at Hoylake, England. Oddly, given the British hallowed attitude toward amateurism in late Victorian and Edwardian England, this championship never received the same singular designation as The Open. It is not referred to as The Amateur, and in fact until 1922 was considered merely one of many informal amateur competitions held in Great Britain. However, because it was always the most popular among all the others, in 1922 the Royal & Ancient Golf Club of St. Andrews began calling it The British Amateur Championship. At the same time, it "grandfathered" the past events, which made the 1885 tournament the very first one.

First Golfer to Have a Set of Custom-Made Clubs, **King James VI of Scotland,** in 1502. He had a bow maker make a set for him. Amusingly, while James VI was party to a movement to ban the game at that time because it was diverting the attention of warriors from archery practice, he became himself an avid golfer.

First Immigrant American to Win The Open, **Jock Hutchison,** 1921. Scottish born, he made most of his fine career in America.

First Homebred American to Win The British Amateur and Open in the Same Year, **Bobby Jones,** 1930. It was his only victory in that Amateur and was part of his celebrated "Grand Slam," which included victories in the 1930 US and British Opens. It was presumably, also, his last try at the Amateur title, for he had made plans to retire from competitive golf after the 1930 season.

First Winner of US and British Amateur Championships in Same Year, **Lawson Little,** in 1934. It was called the "Little Slam," a play on his name, but also a spin-off of Bobby Jones's Grand Slam (see above). Little repeated the feat the following year.

First Winner to Score All Four Rounds in the 60s, **Greg Norman,** with rounds of 66–68–69–64, 267 (–13), in 1993 at Turnberry GC, Ayrshire, Scotland.

► THE OPEN AND BRITISH AMATEUR MOSTS AND LEASTS

Oldest Winner of The Open, **Roberto DeVicenzo,** who was 44 when he won the 1967 championship. It was his only major title in a career during which he won over two hundred tournaments, big and small, worldwide. He had an opportunity to win the 1968 Masters when he tied Bob Goalby and would play off for the title. But because DeVicenzo signed an incorrect scorecard, which gave him a par-4 on the 17th hole when in fact he made a birdie-3, he finished a stroke behind Goalby. It was one of the sadder moments in golf history and brought to question the validity of the scoring system. More than a few million people saw DeVicenzo make the birdie on the 17th, so why penalize him for a simple mistake made in the heat of an emotional moment.

Youngest Winner of The Open, ("Young") **Tom Morris Jr.,** 17, 1868, at Prestwick.

Youngest to Compete in The Open, ("Young") **Tom Morris Jr.,** 14 years, 4 months, 25 days, in 1865.

Oldest to Compete in The Open, ("Old") **Tom Morris Sr.,** 74 years, 11 months, 25 days, in 1896.

Most Victories in The Open, **Six,** Harry Vardon.

Most Second-Place Finishes in The Open, **Seven,** Jack Nicklaus.

Lowest Single-Round Score in The Open, **63,** Mark Hayes, 1977; Isao Aoki, 1980; Greg Norman, 1986; Paul Broadhurst, 1990; Jodie Mudd, 1991; Nick Faldo, 1993; Payne Stewart, 1993.

Least Likely (or Darkest Dark-Horse) Winner of The Open, **Jack White,** 1904.

Winner of The Open with Longest Surname, **William Auchterlonie,** 1893; **Mark Calcavecchia,** 1989.

Heaviest Winner of The Open, **John Daly,** 220 pounds.

Largest Winning Margin in The Open **(since 1900), Eight strokes,** John H. Taylor, 1900; James Braid, 1908; Harry Vardon, 1914; Tiger Woods, 2000.

Lowest Absolute Winning Score, **267 (−13),** Greg Norman, 1993, at Royal St. George's.

Most Consecutive Birdies in The Open, **Seven,** by Christy O'Connor Jr., 1985, at Royal St. George's. He shot a 64. He did not win the championship.

Biggest Comeback to Win The Open, **Thirteen strokes,** George Duncan, in 1920. He shot 71 to make up the thirteen strokes on Abe Mitchell, who helped him out by shooting 84. In the playoff, Duncan won by two strokes over Alexander Herd.

Most Appearances in The Open, **Forty-six,** Gary Player (1956–2001).

Oldest Competitor in The Open, **Gene Sarazen,** 71 years old, in 1973. Sarazen wasn't a factor in the tournament, of course, and he missed the cut, but before that he made a hole-in-one on the famed Postage Stamp hole at Royal Troon GC. The old champ went out in style.

Most Times Host Course of The Open, **Twenty-eight,** St. Andrews, (as of 2010).

Longest Open Course (to Date), **Carnoustie GC,** at 7,421 yards, in 2007.

First American-Born Winner of the British Amateur, **Jesse Sweetser,** 1926.

Youngest British Amateur Champion, **Matteo Mannasero,** 16, when he won the 2009 championship.

6 **the pga tour**

▷ **FIRSTS**

First "Commercial" Professional Tournament, The "Lakewood Classic," perhaps, or maybe the "**Ocean County Open**," Lakewood, New Jersey, January 1, 1898. Actually, there was no title recorded for the event, which was reported in the January 2, 1898, edition of the *New York Times.* In any case, it was the first tournament for professional golfers sponsored by a commercial enterprise. This would be, and remains, the foundation of the pro tour—staging tournaments to gain publicity and enhance the sale of commercial goods. The Tour also grew on the sponsorship of tournaments by Chambers of Commerce of cities and towns seeking tourists, new residents, or businesses, which amounts to the same thing. This is in contrast to championships staged by nonprofit golf organizations such as the United States Golf Association and the Royal & Ancient Golf Association, whose mission is (or has been) to create and administer the rules of the game and through its various championships promote golf for itself.

The Lakewood Classic was put on by a group of hoteliers in what was then a popular resort area between New York City and Atlantic City. Golf was just being introduced to the United States

61

at the time and gaining some popularity, enough that the hotel operators in Lakewood thought they might use it to entertain guests on hand, and, as the tournament was expected to be written up in newspapers, would by virtue of the publicity attract new business.

It was a one-day, thirty-six-hole event over a nine-hole course that was frozen solid. (Lakewood was surrounded by pine tree forests that were said to ameliorate the cold winter air and make outdoor activities feasible. It didn't quite work out that way in this instance.) Ten professionals entered, and Val Fitzjohn defeated his brother, Ed, on the first hole of a playoff to win 50 percent of the $150 total purse. Both shot rounds of 92–88 to get into the playoff.

There was no great profusion of like tournaments in the next year or two, but as soon as Henry Flagler, a onetime business associate of John D. Rockefeller, who is credited with developing Florida as a tourist destination, extended his railroad line into Florida in the late 1880s, new resort hotels, including those he built, began staging tournaments for the same reason the folks in Lakewood did. Golf professionals in the East and Midwest, whose clubs closed down for the winter, would begin to travel south on their winter vacation and play in a gradually increasing numbers of tournaments that in time would be called the winter tour. Eventually, it expanded to cover the entire country and become The Tour.

First Professional Golfer, **Walter Hagen**. This designation is differentiated from that of golf professional, who holds a salaried job at a club or course, gives lessons, sells and repairs equipment, etc., and may occasionally play in tournaments. Until Hagen, all professionals were in this category, even the most successful tournament players. The flamboyant Hagen, however, had no intention of doing this sort of thing with his life. After making his big-time competitive debut in the 1913 US Open (he tied for fourth), Hagen went forth to earn his living only playing the game, mainly by way of exhibitions, but also competing in the important championships and also on the gradually developing pro tournament circuit. He held one head professional job, at Oakland Hills CC in Detroit, while the course was being completed. When it opened for play, Hagen quit the post.

First Manager (Unofficial) of the PGA Tour, Hal Sharkey, 1929. A sportswriter for the *Newark (NJ) News*, Sharkey was asked by noted pros on his beat, including Tommy Armour, Craig Wood, and Bobby Cruickshank, to travel to the West Coast while on his winter vacation and get sponsors of open tournaments out there to schedule their events so there was a logical geographic progression. At the time there would be a tournament in Los Angeles one week, the next week in San Francisco, the next back south in Tijuana. They also asked Sharkey to dicker for reduced hotel rates, help sponsors publicize their events, and drum up more tournaments. A few of the wives of the touring pros had been doing this work, but as the circuit began to develop it needed a more professional director. Sharkey did the job for one winter, but he contracted pneumonia and died. Bob Harlow replaced him. (See below.)

First Salaried, Official Manager of the PGA Tour, Bob Harlow, 1930. After Hal Sharkey's demise, Harlow came on as the salaried manager of the pro tournament circuit. He shaped the operational groundwork for what the Tour has become, and in that respect he can be considered the Father of the PGA Tour. Harlow, a graduate of the University of Pennsylvania and a journalist by profession, got into golf as Walter Hagen's manager. With his background as a newspaperman, connections made handling

Hagen's business affairs, and his particular love of the theater, especially musicals, Harlow was just the man to put the pro tour on a firm foundation. He refined Sharkey's geographic ordering of events, was a master of promotion techniques, and as an articulate, businesswise gentleman of the world, was able to generate new tournaments and raise the purse money to new heights, even during the dog days of the Great Depression.

When the operation of the PGA Tour was taken over by the PGA of America in 1935, Harlow became the *First Official Manager of the Tour*. But he soon ran into personal problems with the president of the PGA of America, George Jacobus, and was relieved of his duties. In the terminology of our time, he left to seek other opportunities. One was founding *Golf World* magazine, in 1947, which has been in continuous publication ever since.

First Commissioner of the PGA Tour, **Joseph P. Dey Jr.** Dey had been the executive secretary of the USGA for thirty-four years before taking on this post. Dey was hired for the position so as to give the newly formed PGA Tour, which had made a bitter separation from its longtime administrative arm, the PGA of America, an image of respectability. Dey projected an air of propriety and moral certitude. He held the post for six years and was replaced by Deane Beman.

First Pro Tour Event Played for Charity, **The Palm Beach Round Robin**, 1938. Golf had been used before to raise money for good causes: during World War I Bobby Jones, "Chick" Evans, and other star players of the time played exhibitions to raise money for the Red Cross. But the famous cure-for-polio March of Dimes campaign initiated by President Franklin D. Roosevelt gave pro tournament golf its essential grounding in charity, albeit with perhaps a bit of political chicanery on the side.

In 1932, Henry Doherty, head of Cities Service Utilities and owner of the Miami-Biltmore Hotel, was having federal tax problems. Bob Harlow, manager of the Tour (see above), and Carl Byoir, a pioneer in the field of public relations, knew that a spa in the town of Warm Springs, Georgia, was having financial difficulties. It was where President Roosevelt was taking the waters that he hoped would cure his polio. Putting two and two together, Harlow and Byoir had a notion that if Doherty put on a big pro tournament at his Miami hotel and turned the profits over to the Warm Springs Spa to fix it up for their most famous guest, Doherty's tax problems might be eased. And they were. Whether FDR had anything to do with that is not clear.

In any case, the Miami-Biltmore Open was staged with a then very impressive $10,000 total purse, and the profits were distributed to the Warm Springs Spa. This led to the realization that a golf tournament with a worthy charity getting the profits was a fine way to generate interest in and expand the pro tour. For one thing, it appealed to the altruism of people to volunteer their help in putting on the tournament proper. This, combined with the fact that no taxes would have to be paid on the profits, set in stone a basic foundation of the modern-day PGA Tour.

However, the first tournament to be played with the announced purpose of raising money for charity was the 1938 Palm Beach Round Robin, sponsored by Elmer Ward, president of the Goodall Company, a clothing manufacturer. The inaugural was played at the Kenwood CC in Cincinnati, Ohio. The profits were given to a hospital on Long Island, New York. It's with this tournament that the PGA Tour's charity record begins. Currently, the Tour claims to have raised well over a billion dollars for charity.

First Time Caddies Wore the Name of Their Player on Their Back, 1938. At the above mentioned Palm Beach Round Robin, in Cincinnati, Ohio.

First Hollywood Movie Star to Sponsor a Tour Event, **Richard Arlen**, who put up the $5,000 purse for the 1932 Los Angeles

Open. It was in the worst times of the Great Depression, and the Los Angeles Chamber of Commerce was unable to raise a purse for this traditional "opening day" of the winter circuit. Arlen, who appeared in over 140 movies during his career, including silents, was a golf buff. He effectively put in motion sponsorship, or at least the name association with pro tournaments by show business personalities. In 1937, Bing Crosby began sponsoring a tournament that eventually grew into the Bing Crosby Pro-Am, which is now the AT&T Pebble Beach National Pro-Am. Other celebrated entertainers would also get similarly involved—Dean Martin, Andy Williams, Sammy Davis, Glen Campbell, Jackie Gleason, and others.

First to Fly His Own Plane on the PGA Tour, **Johnny Bulla**, who played the Tour from the late 1930s into the 1950s. He began flying his plane before World War II. During the war he was a copilot for Eastern Airlines, and after the war bought a DC-3 and flew from one tournament site to the next, taking along, for a fare, up to twenty pros and their wives per flight.

First Son of a Tour Pro to Win on Tour, **Guy Boros**, youngest son of two-time US Open champion, Julius. In 1996, Guy won the Vancouver Open.

First Tour Pro to Knock Himself Out (or at Least Down) with His Putter, **Ivan Gantz**, who played the pro tour sporadically during the 1950s. He didn't accomplish much as a player, but he gained a legendary reputation for his temper. Witnesses reported that on more than a few occasions Ivan often whacked himself in the head with his putter after missing a short putt and at least put himself down for the count. Ivan refuted the latter event, admitting he sent himself reeling against the ropes more than once but that he was never knocked off his feet.

First Pro Tour Event in Pacific Northwest, **The Seattle Open,** 1936. Macdonald Smith won in a playoff against Ralph Guldahl.

First Official Leading Money Winner on the PGA Tour, **Paul Runyan,** 1934, with $6,767.

First Vardon Trophy Winner by Average Strokes Per Round, **Jimmy Demaret,** 1947. The Vardon Trophy was inaugurated in 1934 with a point system; the first winner in that format was Harry Cooper. The system was changed in 1947 to single-round stroke average. In 1988 there was a further change that required the winner to have played a minimum of sixty rounds.

The First Vardon Trophy Winner under the Current System, **Chip Beck,** with 69.46, in 1988.

First Amateur to Win a US Pro Tour Event, **Bobby Jones,** Southeastern Open, 1930. Jones usually prepared for competitive golf every year by playing informal rounds with friends; he was not a range rat who beat out a lot of balls into an open field. However, in 1930, while not saying as much in public, he did confide to close friends that this year he was going to try to win the four major championships of the time—the US and British Open and Amateur championships—what would be called The Grand Slam. No one had ever done it, and this would be Jones's last chance, as he was planning to retire from competitive golf at the end of the year. With that goal in mind Jones broke with his usual pattern and entered a couple of early-year pro tour tournaments, the Savannah Open and the Southeastern, in Augusta, Georgia. At Savannah he finished second by one stroke to Horton Smith, who was the hottest player on the pro tour at the time. In the Southeastern Jones swamped the field, finishing thirteen strokes ahead of runner-up Smith. Then, of course, he went on to do the Grand Slam.

Interesting coincidences here. It was in Augusta where Jones would found the Augusta National Golf Club and the Masters tournament. And it was Horton Smith who won the inaugural Masters, in 1934 (and the third one, as well).

First Five-Figure Total Purse, **The 1926 Los Angeles Open**, with a total purse of $10,000. Harry Cooper won the tournament and collected the $3,500 first prize. He won it again in 1937, during the Great Depression, and collected $2,500.

First Five-Figure Winner's Prize, **$10,000**, to Gene Sarazen when he won the Agua Caliente Open, 1930. The money was delivered in a wheelbarrow full of silver dollars. At least for the photo op.

First Winner with a Score under 270 for Seventy-two Holes, **Ky Laffoon**, won the 1934 Park Hill Open in Denver with a score of 266.

First to Shoot Four Rounds under Seventy and Not Win, **Jimmy Demaret**, in the 1942 Hale America National Open. Demaret had rounds of 68–68–69–69–274, but lost to Ben Hogan, who had rounds of 72–62–69–68–271.

First Round of 60, **Al Brosch**, in 1951 Texas Open, at the Brackenridge GC, San Antonio. It was 11–under par on a public course that gave up two other 60s—by Ted Kroll, in 1954, and Mike Souchak, in 1955. Souchak's 60 helped him to set the seventy-two-hole scoring record of 257 that held up for forty-six years. The second player chronologically to shoot a 60 (–11) was Bill Nary, who did it in the third round of the 1952 El Paso Open. An interesting story goes with this one. Nary told me that when warming up for the record-tying round he shanked every iron he hit. He began his session on the left side of the range, but after four shanks the pros to the right of him told him he better move to the far right side of the practice area. Which he did. He then went out and played a flawless round of golf, which proves that you don't always want to take your practice shots to the first tee, assuming you hit them well; or, hitting them poorly focuses your attention on not doing so.

First Pro to Play a Tour Event Wearing Shorts, **Jimmy Demaret**, in the 1947 Tam O'Shanter All-American tournament. Demaret was a style-conscious player who effectively changed the way golfers dressed for the game. He was a free-spirited man who foreswore the drab, heavy clothing golfers had been playing in for centuries and began wearing loose-fitting, colorful shirts and pants, three-tone shoes, and various styles of hats worn at rakish angles. While most other pros did not follow his lead in terms of colors, the more comfortable clothing Demaret introduced did become the norm in golf. In keeping with his outré manner, Demaret appeared on the tee of the 1947 Tam O'Shanter event wearing shorts. In fact, another pro, Freddie Haas Jr., joined him in the apparel breakthrough. However, it had an abbreviated life if only because Demaret's pair was tight-fitting short shorts. Jimmy had a substantial tush and was rather well fixed up front, and he was asked not to wear the shorts for the sake of propriety, or good taste. He complied. While at the time no official directive against shorts was sent out by tour officials, it eventually became a PGA Tour rule.

First Professional Athlete from Another Sport to Win on the PGA Tour, **Sam Byrd**, 1942, Greater Greensboro Open. Byrd played eight seasons in the major leagues, six with the New York Yankees, two with the Cincinnati Reds. When a Yankee he was referred to as "Babe Ruth's Legs" because in the late innings of games, when Ruth was near the end of his playing days, Byrd often ran for Ruth when he reached base, or simply went into right field for Ruth to finish out games.

Byrd had a .274 career batting average, with one year over .300 (.312). He won a total of six times on the PGA Tour and lost four and three in the final match of the 1945 PGA Championship to Byron Nelson (this was one of Nelson's eleven consecutive victories streak). Nelson once said of Byrd that he was one of the best long-irons players he ever saw.

After his playing career, Byrd taught golf, mainly at a self-owned driving range in Birmingham, Alabama. His most notable student was Jimmy Ballard, who became a well-known teacher and taught the Byrd method to the likes of Curtis Strange, Hal Sutton, and Sandy Lyle, among others. The "method" had a lot of baseball in it.

First Tennis Champion to Play on the Pro Tour, **Ellsworth Vines,** a World Number One or co-Number One tennis champion in the early 1930s, winner of the Wimbledon and the USLTA Championship. Vines turned golf pro in his late twenties and won once, the 1946 Massachusetts Open. However, several times in the 1940s he finished high on the annual money-winning list, and in 1951 went to the semifinals of the PGA Championship, losing to Walter Burkemo on the 37th hole.

First Indian to Play the PGA Tour, **Rajun Atwal.** Vijay Singh is of Indian descent, but he is a native of Fiji and is "registered" as Fijian.

First Native American to Play the PGA Tour, **Rod Curl,** a full-blooded Wintu from Redding, California, who played the tour from 1969 through 1978. He won once, defeating Jack Nicklaus by a stroke in the 1974 Colonial National Invitational, and overall had forty-two top-ten finishes.

First Movie Star to Play on the PGA Tour, **Joe Kirkwood Jr.,** who was best known for playing Joe Palooka in the movies. Palooka was a boxer born in the newspaper comic strips. Kirkwood's father was a golf professional best known as a trick-shot artist.

First Left-Hander to Win a PGA Tour Event as an Amateur, **Phil Mickelson.** The 1991 Northern Telcom Open.

First Winner of the Players Championship, **Jack Nicklaus,** 1974, with a 272 (−16) at the Atlanta CC, in Marietta, Georgia. The tournament is meant to be the showcase championship of the PGA Tour, the organization of the touring pros that was formed in 1968 when those who played exclusively tournament golf split from the PGA of America, which had long administered the tournament circuit. The Players Championship has all the qualifications of a "major" title, especially after it moved to its permanent site, TPC Sawgrass, in Ponte Vedra, Florida (where the PGA Tour has its headquarters), and may one day be conferred as such.

First International Winner of the Players Championship, **Sandy Lyle,** 1987.

First Australian Winner of the Players Championship, **Steve Elkington,** 1991.

First Zimbabwean Winner of the Players Championship, **Nick Price,** 1993.

First Asian (South Korea) Winner of the Players Championship, **K. J. Choi,** 2011.

First Spanish Winner of the Players Championship, **Sergio Garcia,** 2008.

First Swedish Winner of the Players Championship, **Henrik Stenson,** 2009.

First New Zealand Winner of the Players Championship, **Craig Perks,** 2002.

Most Second-Place Finishes in the Players Championship, Jack Nicklaus, **Three** (1974, 1976, 1978).

First (and So Far Only) Winner of a Pro Tournament Putting with Only One Hand, Joe Turnesa, 1926 Metropolitan (New York) Open. He used only his right (dominant) hand. He did not continue putting that way, despite the success. Mike Hulbert putted with his right hand for six months on the 1995 PGA Tour, without a victory, although he remarked that it was one of the best runs he ever had on the circuit. Tiger Woods, among others, does a lot of practice putting using only his right hand. It is based on the Dominant-Hand theory, whereby a right-handed person (or left-handed) uses that hand to control the key aspects of putting—distance, line—leaving the opposite hand only to stabilize the club during the stroke.

First Winner of a PGA Tour Event Using a Long Putter, **Rocco Mediate,** 1991 Doral-Ryder Open.

First Winner of a Tour Event Using a Metal-Head Driver, **Ron Streck,** 1981 Michelob-Houston Open. (See more under **Equipment.**)

First Winner of a Major Using a Metal-Head Driver, **Lee Trevino,** 1984 PGA Championship.

First National Hockey League Player to Play the PGA Tour, **Bill Ezinicki,** who played for the Toronto Maple Leafs, Boston Bruins, and New York Rangers in the late 1940s to early 1950s. He turned to golf after retiring from hockey and played the PGA Tour periodically. He was head pro at The International GC in Bolton, Massachusetts, and he won nine regional (Northeast) Opens, including those in Rhode Island, New Hampshire, Massachusetts, and Maine. He was elected into the New England Section of the PGA Hall of Fame in 1997. Another former hockey player, Stan Mikita, a star with the Chicago Blackhawks, turned golf professional after retiring from hockey and became the head professional at the Kemper Lakes GC, outside Chicago. Hockey players have generally been very adept at golf. After all, the stroke is essentially the same for hitting an object off the ground. Indeed, there is considerable evidence to suggest that golf really began in Holland, where they played a game on frozen ponds that was called kolf. It has been speculated that the Scots picked up the Dutch game and instead played on grass, with the aim of putting a ball into a hole in the ground. The first golf clubs in Scotland were woods, shaped very much like the sticks used by the Dutch kolfers.

▶ MOSTS

Most Top-Ten Finishes (Career), **358**, Sam Snead.

Most Top-Ten Finishes in a Season, **Fifty-one**, Harold "Jug" Mc-Spaden, in 1945. McSpaden set this mark in the year that Byron Nelson set his records for eleven straight victories and total of eighteen victories for the year. McSpaden was second best that year, and because there were so many Nelson-McSpaden one-two finishes they were dubbed "The Gold Dust Twins."

Most Victories in a Calendar Year, **Eighteen**, Byron Nelson, 1945.

Most Consecutive Victories on the PGA Tour, **Eleven**, Byron Nelson, 1945. This is one record that may never be broken. There is a personal disclaimer, however. One of the victories was in the Miami Four-Ball, in which Byron had a partner—"Jug" McSpaden, who was the second-best player in golf in 1945. McSpaden must have helped some in that victory. Therefore, we put Byron's record at 10½. So sue me.

Most Victories on PGA Tour, **Eighty-three,** Sam Snead. His total stood at eighty-four for many years, but in 1986, after a review ordered by Deane Beman, commissioner of the PGA Tour, the total was reduced to eighty-two. However, in 2011 an astute golf fan in England named Martin Davies informed me that Snead's victory in the 1949 North & South Open was not recorded as an official victory by the PGA Tour. Odd, because the North & South was at least a semimajor during its entire run, which dates from 1902 to 1951. Snead was very unhappy with the decision to reduce his number from eighty-four, but we now have some redemption for him.

First, transparency. Yours truly was a member of the committee that dropped three of Snead's victories, all of them events with small fields and played on Sam's home course, the Greenbrier Resort. One event was later added to his record, the 1947 British Open, which made his official total eighty-two. Others on the committee included Herbert Warren Wind, Jay Hebert, Joseph P. Dey, Joe Black and Jack Tuthill. We didn't take enough time in our judgments. The three tournaments we shot down were done so on the basis of the total purse, which was a criteria in the 1930s and 1940s for a Tour event being "official." We didn't consider the quality of the field in each, which was about as good as they could be even if smaller than usual. And of course, we missed altogether the 1949 North & South Open.

In any case, after hearing from Mr. Davies, I checked with the PGA Tour on the 1949 North & South and why it was not counted as an official victory for Snead. I was told it was deemed unofficial in 1947, 1948, and 1949, but a reason was not given. One criterion for unofficialness in those days was the size of the purse, and presumably a $7,500 total purse in 1949 was under the limit, hence unofficial. However, in 1950 the purse was exactly the same and this one was deemed official. Snead having won it again was (is) counted on his official record. Another criterion was the quality of the field. In 1949, as in all North & South tournaments, it was a full field (111 players) and excellent. It included Cary Middlecoff, who won the US Open that year, Julius Boros, Clayton Heafner, and many other top-of-the-line tour players. The quality of the course was another criterion. The North & South was played on the famed Pinehurst #2, one of the best in the world. It ran to 6,952 yards in 1949. Therefore, we hereby confer official status on the 1949 North & South Open and up Snead's "official" total to eighty-three.

Most Consecutive Cuts Made (Career) on PGA Tour (as of 2007), Tiger Woods.

Most Consecutive Birdies, **Nine**, Mark Calcavecchia, 2009 Canadian Open. He tied for 8th.

Highest Score on a Single Hole, **Twenty-three**, by Tommy Armour on a par-5 during the 1927 Shawnee Open, at Shawnee-on-the-Delaware, Pennsylvania. At 18 over the par, it was called an Archaeopteryx. Why that designation is unclear, except to say the archaeopteryx is an ancient bird believed to have evolved from the dinosaur. Armour, who studied at Edinburgh University, might have given it that name. Ironically, Armour accomplished this feat a week after winning the US Open.

Highest Score on a Par-4 Hole, **Sixteen**, by Kevin Na, a South Korean-born PGA Tour player, in the first round of the 2011 Texas Open. On the 9th hole of the TPC San Antonio GC, in San Antonio, Na hit his tee shot into an unplayable lie. He went back to tee and hit his third shot in almost exactly the same place as he hit the first one. Not allowed to take another unplayable lie, he took a drop and a whack at his ball, which ricocheted back and hit him in the leg. That cost him another penalty stroke. He now lay five. The next shot barely moved. He then took a series of strokes very quickly. One went sideways; another went backwards. He swung at one left-handed (he's a righty) and moved the ball a foot or so. He tried another left-handed swing, with a similar result. After another two strokes from an off-balance stance he finally lifted his ball just over a tree branch. Now with a decent swing from the rough, he played his 14th shot to the back fringe of the green. Two putts later he recorded a 12 over par-16. He finished the round with an 8-over-par 80. Admirably, he played the back nine in 3–under par. The next day he shot a 77, and of course, missed the cut.

Most Birdies over Seventy-two Holes on PGA Tour, **Thirty-two,** by Mark Calcavecchia, in the 2001 Phoenix Open. He won the tournament, by two strokes. Paul Gow, 2001 B.C. Open.

Oldest First-Time Winner on PGA Tour, **John Barnum,** at 51 years, 1 month, 5 days, when winning the 1962 Cajun Classic.

Oldest Winner on the PGA Tour, **Sam Snead,** the 1965 Greater Greensboro Open, at age 52 years, 10 months, 8 days.

Oldest to Make Cut in a PGA Tour Event, **Sam Snead,** who was 67 years, 2 months, 21 days, at the 1979 Westchester Classic. He tied for 47th.

Oldest Top-Ten Finisher on PGA Tour, **Sam Snead,** 63 years, 3 months, 4 days, in 1975 B.C. Open.

Oldest to Make Cut in a Major, **Sam Snead,** 67 years, 2 months, 7 days, 1979 PGA Championship (T42nd).

Oldest Top-Ten Finisher in a Major, **Sam Snead,** 62 years, 2 months, 15 days, 1974 PGA Championship.

Oldest to Shoot His Age (or Better) in a PGA Tour Event, **Sam Snead,** in 1979 Quad Cities Open. 67-year-old Sam Snead shot a

67 in the third round and beat his age with a 66 in the fourth and final round. However, he did not win the tournament.

Player Suffering Most Losses to a Hole-Out on the Final Hole of a Tournament, **Greg Norman,** four. Bob Tway holed from a greenside bunker on the 72nd hole of the 1986 PGA Championship for a birdie three; in a sudden-death playoff for the 1987 Masters, Larry Mize holed a pitch-and-run on the 11th hole (second of the playoff) for a birdie three; in the 1990 Nestle Invitational Robert Gamez holed a 7-iron second shot on the 18th hole for an eagle two; in the 1990 USF&G Classic, David Frost holed out from a greenside bunker on the 18th hole for a birdie.

Most Tour Events Played without a Victory, **357 (to date),** Michael Allen. Allen joined the PGA Tour in 1988, and though without a win on the major circuit, he has won over $5 million in prize money. And, he has won elsewhere—once on the Nationwide Tour (1998 Greater Austin Open), once overseas (1989 Bell's Scottish Open), and most notably, once on the Champion Tour (2009 Senior PGA Championship).

Longest Sudden-Death Playoff to a Decision, **Eight holes,** on four different occasions: Dick Hart defeated Phil Rodgers in the 1965 Azalea Open; Lee Elder defeated Lee Trevino in the 1978 Milwaukee Open; Dave Barr defeated Woody Blackburn, Dan Halldorson, Frank Conner, and Victor Regalado in the 1981 Quad Cities Open; Bob Gilder defeated Rex Caldwell, Johnny Miller, and Mark O'Meara in the 1981 Phoenix Open.

Longest Sudden-Death Playoff in Which No One Died (Lost), **Eleven holes,** Lloyd Mangrum and Cary Middlecoff went that many in overtime in an effort to decide the winner of the 1949 Motor City Open. Exhausted, and with darkness coming on, both players agreed to be co-champions and split first and second money.

Most Victories in a Single Event, **Eight,** the Greensboro Open, by Sam Snead.

Most Cuts Made (Career), **592,** Jay Haas.

Most Consecutive Cuts Made (Career), **142,** Tiger Woods.

Most Under Par for Thirty-six Holes, **Steve Stricker** (−21 on rounds of 61–62), in the 2009 Bob Hope Classic. Stricker also holds the record for *Most Strokes Under Par for Seventy-two Holes,* **Thirty-three,** at the same tournament. Stricker shot a 77 in the fifth and final round of the ninety-hole event and tied for third.

Most Consecutive Birdies in a PGA Tour Event, **Nine,** Mark Calcavecchia, in the second round of the 2009 Canadian Open. He finished the tournament tied for 8th.

Most Consecutive Birdies to Win a PGA Tour Event, **Eight,** Bob Goalby, "Fuzzy" Zoeller. Goalby's streak led to a final-round 65 and victory in the 1961 St. Petersburg Open. Zoeller's run led to a first round 63 in the 1976 Quad Cities Open.

Most Consecutive Years Winning at Least One Tournament, **Seventeen,** Jack Nicklaus (1962–1978); Arnold Palmer (1955–1971).

Longest Putt Holed in a PGA Tour Event, **110 feet,** Jack Nicklaus in the 1964 Tournament of Champions.

Most Wins in the Players Championship, **Jack Nicklaus** (1974, 1976, 1978).

Most Pungent Advice Given a Golfer with a Clutch Shot to Play. In the 1953 Tam O'Shanter World Championship, at the Tam O'Shanter CC, Niles, Illinois, Lew Worsham needed a birdie three on the last (72nd) hole to tie Chandler Harper and force a playoff for the $25,000 first prize (the biggest winner's purse ever offered in golf up to that time). Worsham was in the last pairing of the day and had a 118-yard shot to a green set behind a ten-yard-wide creek. There was no way to play around the creek. Worsham chose a wedge (a MacGregor Double-Duty model) for the shot, and as he was beginning to set up to play the ball his caddy, a typically direct Chicagoan from the nabes, told his man: "Remember pro, the water in that creek ain't frozen." With that in mind Worsham hit the ball into the cup for an eagle two and an outright victory.

▶ LEASTS

Fewest Putts in a Round, **Eighteen,** Sam Trahan, 1979 IV Philadelphia Golf Classic; Mike McGee, 1987 Federal Express St. Jude Classic; Kenny Knox, 1989 MCI Heritage Classic; Andy North, 1990 Anheuser Busch Golf Classic; Jim McGovern, 1992 Federal Express St. Jude Classic; Corey Pavin, 2000 Bell Canadian Open; Ken Duke, 2009 World Golf Championship; Blake Adams, 2010.

Lowest Vardon Trophy Stroke Average, **67.79,** Tiger Woods, 2000 (76 rounds).

Fewest Putts over Seventy-two Holes, **Ninety-two,** David Frost, at the 2005 Heritage Classic.

Fewest Putts over Nine Holes, **Six,** by Stan Utley in 2002 Air Canada Championship.

Lowest Competitive Round on the PGA Tour, **Fifty-nine,** by Al Geiberger, in second round of 1977 Memphis Open at Colonial CC (par-72); Chip Beck, in third round of 1991 Las Vegas Invitational on Sunrise GC (par-72); David Duval, in final round of 1999 Bob Hope Chrysler Classic, at PGA West, Palmer course (par-72); Paul Goydos, in 2010 John Deere Classic, Silvis, Illinois, TPC Deere Run GC (par-71); Stuart Appleby, in 2010 Greenbrier Classic, White Sulphur Springs, West Virginia, Old White course (par-70).

Geiberger's round might have gotten an asterisk because the course was very wet from heavy rains and preferred lies in the fairways was the order of the day. However, Geiberger told me he never took advantage of the ruling because he hit every fairway in regulation and found no need to take a lie. The fairways were in Bermuda grass and, although wet, the ball sat up nicely on them.

Three of the 59-shooters won the tournament in which they shot the record score—Geiberger, Duval, and Appleby. Duval and Appleby shot their 59 in the final round. Duval won outright, but Appleby had to go into a playoff. Beck finished third, Goydos second. With 59s! Tough game!

Smallest Winning Purse on the PGA Tour, $400, to Joe Turnesa when he won the 1931 Miami Open. The Great Depression was beginning to deepen at this time, and money for professional golf tournaments was hard to come by. In this tournament, which for many years was a regular date on the tour, the total purse came from the players' entry fees, gate receipts, and a $500 contribution from a local businessman.

Smallest Amount of Money Earned in a Tournament, $37.14, in the 1951 Miami Open. Seven players tied for 16th, the last money place, and split $259.99. They were Lloyd Wadkins, Felice Torza, Chuck Klein, Otey Crisman, Julius Boros, Lew Worsham, and Jimmy Demaret. Actually, there was an extra penny and Demaret got it because he wore the most colorful clothes or was last man off the course, or won a flip of the penny; it is uncertain.

Lowest Total Winning Score (Seventy-two Holes, Par-70 course), 254 (–26), by Tommy Armour III (in the 2003 Texas Open, at The Resort at La Cantera, San Antonio, Texas). Armour III's grandfather was the famed "Silver Scot," the great champion player and noted golf teacher.

Lowest Total Winning Score (Seventy-two Holes, Par-71 course), **256 (−28)**, by Mark Calcavecchia, in the 2001 Phoenix Open, at TPC Scottsdale GC.

Lowest Total Winning Score (Seventy-two Holes, Par-72 course), **260 (−28)**, by John Huston, 1998 Hawaiian Open, Waialae CC; Phil Mickelson, 2006 Bell South Classic, TPC at Sugarloaf—Stable and Meadows courses—Duluth, Georgia.

Lowest Total for Consecutive Rounds in a PGA Tour Event, **189**, by Chandler Harper (63–63–63–24) in the 2nd, 3rd, and 4th rounds of the 1954 Texas Open at the Brackenridge Park GC, San Antonio (par-71); by John Cook (64–62–63, -24) in the 1st, 2nd, and 3rd rounds of the 1996 FedEx St. Jude Classic, at the TPC Southwind GC, Memphis, Tennessee (par-71); Mark Calcavecchia (65–60–64, -24) in the 1st, 2nd, and 3rd rounds of the 2001 Phoenix Open, at the TPC Scottsdale GC (par-71); Tommy Armour III (64–62–63, -21) in the 1st, 2nd, and 3rd rounds of the 2003 Valero Texas Open, at The Resort at LaCantera GC (par-70), San Antonio.

Shortest Putt Missed on PGA Tour, **One inch**, by Bill Nary, 1949 Rio Grande Open.

Lowest Total Score for Nine Holes in a PGA Tour Event, **26 (−8)**, by Corey Pavin, in the US Bank Championship in Milwaukee, on the Brown Deer Park GC (par-34).

Lowest Number of Strokes Under Par for Nine Holes in a PGA Tour Event, **Nine**, by Billy Mayfair, with a 27 on the back nine (par-36) in the 2001 Buick Open, at the Warwick Hills G&CC, Detroit; Robert Gamez, with a 27 on the front nine (par-36) in the 2004 Bob Hope Chrysler Classic, at the Indian Wells CC, Palm Springs, California.

Youngest Player to Make the Cut in a PGA Tour Event, **Bob Pana-siuk**, Canadian Open. He was 15 years, 8 months, and 20 days old.

Largest Winning Margin in a PGA Tour Event, **Sixteen strokes**, by J. Douglas Edgar, in the 1919 Canadian Open; Joe Kirkwood Sr., the 1924 Corpus Christi Open (Kirkwood was best known, and made his living, as a trick-shot artist, but obviously had plenty of regular game); Bobby Locke, the 1948 Chicago Victory National Open.

Lowest Winning Score in the Players Championship, **264 (–24)**, Greg Norman, 1994.

Youngest Player to Qualify for a PGA Tour Card, **Ty Tryon**, at age 17, in 2001.

Youngest Player to Compete in a PGA Tour Event, **Michelle Wie**, at age 14, in the 2004 Sony Open, in Hawaii. Wie, a prodigal woman golfer from Hawaii, turned professional at 16 (in 2005) and plays on the LPGA tournament circuit.

7 senior pga tour

▶ FIRSTS, MOSTS, AND LEASTS

First Unofficial Senior PGA Tour Event, **1978 Legends of Golf**, a Two-Man-Team Best-Ball competition created by Fred Raphael, the producer of the Emmy Award–winning television series *Shell's Wonderful World of Golf.* Shown on national television, and won by the team of Sam Snead and Gardner Dickinson, the Legends tournament let the world of golf know that pro golfers over 50 years of age still had plenty of game and were fun to watch. The second year is when that perception truly took hold. In a playoff, the team of Julius Boros and Roberto DeVicenzo played Tommy Bolt and Art Wall Jr. and had a terrific duel with the rambunctious and colorful Bolt trading birdies with a smiling, avuncular DeVicenzo. With every birdie they both gesticulated their competitive enthusiasm. It was so well received that Snead, Dickinson, Boros, and some other seniors put together a tournament circuit that blossomed into the Senior PGA Tour (now known as the Champions Tour). The rest is history. (See below.)

First Official Senior PGA Tour Event, **1980 Atlantic City (NJ) International**, won by Don January.

Most Senior Tour events are at fifty-four holes, but a few do play at seventy-two holes. So, the records for each are given where it is pertinent.

Most Victories (to Date), **Forty-five**, Hale Irwin.

Most Victories in a Calendar Year, **Nine**, Peter Thomson, 1985; Hale Irwin, 1997.

Most Consecutive Years Winning at Least One Tournament, **Eleven**, Hale Irwin.

Most Consecutive Years Winning Multiple Tournaments, **Eleven**, Hale Irwin.

Largest Winning Margin (Seventy-two Holes), **Twelve**, Hale Irwin, in the 1997 PGA Seniors Championship. *(Fifty-four Holes)*, **Eleven**, Fred Funk, 2007 Turtle Bay Championship.

Longest Consecutive Birdie Run, **Eight**, by Chi-Chi Rodriguez, Jim Colbert, Dana Quigley, Joe Ozaki.

Most Birdies (Fifty-four Holes), **Twenty-six**, by Loren Roberts in the 2006 MasterCard Championship.

Most Birdies (Seventy-two Holes), **Twenty-eight**, by Jack Nicklaus in the 1990 Mazda Senior Tournament Players Championship.

Most Consecutive Sub-Par Rounds, **Thirty-one**, Gil Morgan, 2000.

Most Consecutive Sub-70 Rounds, **Thirteen**, Hale Irwin, 1999.

Longest Winning Streak, **Four**, Chi-Chi Rodriguez, 1987 Vintage at the Dominion, United Hospitals Classic, Silver Pages Classic, Senior Players Reunion.

Biggest Final-Round Comeback to Victory, **Ten strokes**, Jay Sigel, 1994 GTE West Classic.

Oldest Player to Better His Age, **Harold "Jug" McSpaden**, with an 81 at the age of 85 in the 1994 PGA Seniors' Tournament.

Most Accurate Driving, **Forty-two of Forty-two Fairways,** Calvin Peete, 1996 VFW Senior Championship, Ed Dougherty, 2005 The ACE Classic.

Most Victories in a Single Event, **Six,** Hale Irwin, 1997, 2000 Kaanapali Classic, then the renamed Turtle Bay Championship, 2001, 2002, 2003, 2005.

Longest Drive, **422 yards,** Jim Dent, in 1996 Tradition; Jay Sigel, 1990 Tradition.

Longest Sudden-Death Playoff, **Ten holes,** between Dave Stockton and David Graham, in 1998 Royal Caribbean Classic. Graham won.

Largest Final-Round Comeback for Victory, **Ten strokes,** Jay Sigel, to win the 1994 GTE West Classic.

Most Greens Hit in Regulation over Fifty-four Holes, **Fifty-three,** Brad Bryant, in 2006 Regions Charity Classic.

Lowest Winning Score (Seventy-two Holes), **261(–27),** Jack Nicklaus, with rounds of 65–68–64–64 in the 1990 Mazda Senior.

Lowest Winning Score (Fifty-four Holes), **191 (–19),** Bruce Fleisher, with rounds of 60–64–67 in the 2002 RJR Championship.

Fewest Putts in One Round, **Seventeen,** Bob Brue, 1994 Kroger Senior Classic.

Fewest Putts, Nine Holes, **Seven,** Bob Brue, 1994 Kroger Senior Classic.

Fewest Putts (Fifty-four Holes), **Sixty-nine,** Lee Elder, 1988 Gus Machado Senior Classic.

Best One-Year Scoring Average, **68.59,** Hale Irwin, 1998.

Youngest Player to Shoot His Age, or Better It, **Walter Morgan,** with a 60, at age 61, in the 2002 AT&T Canada Senior Open.

8
miscellaneous

▷ FIRSTS

First Written Reference to Golf, **1457**, when James II of Scotland issued a warning: "Ye fut bawe and ye golf be utterly cryt downe and not usyt." He was concerned that his soldiers were spending too much time at golf and falling behind on their archery practice, which was how they fought foes in those days. Hence, James felt he and his country were in danger from its enemies. However, when James became King James VII of England and Ireland, he took up golf.

First "Regulation" Eighteen-hole Golf Course, **St. Andrews (Old)**. Until 1754 there was no set number of holes comprising a round of golf. Some of the original courses in Scotland had five holes, some had twelve; it all depended on how much ground was available at the site and how long the golfers wanted each hole to play, among other considerations. St. Andrews had twenty-two holes in the beginning. Most of the greens served two holes. For example, the second hole and sixteenth occupy the same stretch of putting surface, so the expanse is big enough that the actual holes can be separated by some fifty yards. In 1754 the powers-that-be at St. Andrews decided to eliminate four holes by eliminating two double-greens closest to the club-house. That left eighteen holes.

As it happened, in 1754 the Royal & Ancient Society of St. Andrews Golfers became the game's official ruling body, and be-cause the most prestigious golf club in the game had an eighteen-hole course, other courses followed suit and a regulation number was set in stone. Thus, eighteen holes have no mythological or symbolic meaning; it became a round of golf by chance, or whim.

***First Official Rules of Golf,* 1744.** Before this date each golf club had its own set of rules, although they were all quite similar. In April 1744, a tournament was going to be played at the Leith Links, and it was deemed necessary by the Gentlemen Golfers of Leith that a universal set of rules be set down on paper for all to see, and obey. They became the first standardized rules of golf. Entitled "Articles & Laws in Playing at Golf," there were thirteen. Scalian Originalists might rule that we should revert to them, but almost all are irrelevant to the way the game has developed. Here are the thirteen, with my commentary. Otherwise, make up your own mind.

1. You must Tee your Ball within a Club's length of the Hole. *(Long out of date, and for good reason. Greens such as they were in those days were nothing more than the fairway with a hole cut into it. As greens became separate entities—larger and of finer or lower-cut grass—playing a tee shot to the next hole from just beside the previous hole would cause severe damage to the putting surface.)*

2. Your tee must be on the Ground. *(Hmmm. Where else would a tee be? Unless, it means you couldn't put your ball up on a mound of sand or dirt, and later a wooden peg, to start play on a hole. If that was the meaning, then of course this rule has been rescinded.)*

3. You are not to change the Ball, which you strike off the Tee. *(The One-Ball rule, which is right up to date.)*

4. You are not to remove Stones, Bones or any Break Club for the sake of playing your Ball, Except upon the fair Green within a Club's length of your Ball. *(Still on the books, sort of; there are no bones these days, even in Scotland's hinterlands. What a break club is, no one seems to know for certain.)*

5. If your Ball comes among watter, or any wattery filth, you are at liberty to take out your Ball & bringing it behind the hazard and Teeing it, you may play it with any Club and allow your Adversary a Stroke for so getting out your Ball. *(Still good.)*

6. If your Balls be found any where touching one another, You are to lift the first Ball, till you play the last. *(Still good, although it doesn't say to mark it before lifting.)*

7. At Holling you are to play your Ball honestly for the Hole, and not to play upon your Adversary's Ball, not laying in your way to. *(Which was meant to promote good sportsmanship and not purposely lay a stymie on your opponent. Since the stymie has been abolished, this rule is redundant.)*

8. If you should lose your Ball, by its being taken up, or any other way, you are to go back to the Spot, where you struck last, & drop another Ball, And allow your adversary a Stroke for the misfortune. *(The Lost Ball rule that holds to this day, although this is worded as though the first rules were designed only for a match-play format. Indeed, in 1759 there were some alterations or accommodations of the rules to account for a stroke-play format.)*

9. No man at Holling his Ball, is to be allowed to mark his way to the Hole with his Club, or anything else. *(This may be*

*the background to why the USGA and R&A were so ada-
mant about the rule forbidding the tapping down of spike
marks. The argument against tapping them down was that
players could create a trench through which they could run
their ball to the hole. A specious argument, to say the least,
if only because there are never that many spike marks in a
line to the hole. And besides, anyone tapping hard enough,
or not in fact tapping a spike mark, could be called out for
inappropriate action. The rule has become moot with the ar-
rival of the plastic cleat and an almost universal barring of
metal spikes.)*

10. If a Ball be stopp'd by any Person, Horse, Dog or anything
    else, the Ball so stop'd must be play'd where it lies. *(Still
    pertains.)*

11. If you draw your Club in Order to Strike, & proceed so far
    in the Stroke as to be bringing down your Club; If then
    your club shall break, in any way, it is to be Accounted a
    Stroke. *(Still pertains.)*

12. He whose Ball lies farthest from the Hole is obliged to play
    first. *(The honors system, which still prevails.)*

13. Neither Trench, Ditch or Dyke made for the preserva-
    tion of the Links, nor the Scholar's Holes, or the Soldier's
    Lines, Shall be accounted a Hazard; But the Ball is to be
    taken out and play'd with any iron Club. *(There have been
    many, many alterations to this rule, and of course there are
    no more Scholar's Holes or Soldier's Lines, whatever they
    may have been.).*

First Reference to the Term Par, 1870. The word itself is from
the stock market. To wit, "A stock may be above or below its
proper, normal or par figure [price]." It came to be applied to

golf when A. H. Doleman, a writer for the British magazine *Golf*, asked two Scottish professionals what score would be required to win The Belt, which was the prize for winning what was, in effect, the British Open. It was to be played at the Prestwick course, as were the previous ten such tournaments, and when it was still a twelve-hole layout. The pros, Davie Strath and Jamie Anderson, said that perfect play should produce a score of 49. Doleman called this "par" for the course. Young Tom Morris won the tournament with a thirty-six-hole score of 149, two over the par, and the term stuck.

Doleman also suggested that determining the par for a hole should be based on how the majority of first-class players score on holes. He fleshed this out by calculating the length of the holes according to the driving power of a first-class player and allowing two putts per hole. Thus, a hole that can be reached in one stroke will be put down as a par-3. And so on.

First Golf Course on European Continent, Pau Golf Club, in Pau, France. It was founded in 1856 and is attributed to the Napoleonic Wars and the 1814 Battle of Ortega. At that time some regiments of Wellington's army were quartered in Pau, and two Scottish soldiers took every opportunity to practice their national game on a makeshift course of their own devising. Twenty years later they returned to Pau, which is in southern France, to vacation and saw the landscape as ideal for a true golf course. It took some years to buy the necessary land, but it got done and hence, the Pau Golf Club was born.

First Eighteen-Hole Golf Course in the United States, Chicago GC, Wheaton, Illinois. Designed by Charles Blair MacDonald, opened in 1894. (See also under **USGA Championships Firsts**.)

The First Golf Club West of the Allegheny Mountains, Chicago GC.

When the Out-of-Bounds Rule Was First Introduced (Rule 27-
1), **1899**. This rule has long been a point of contention among
golfers. The rule is, if a ball is hit out of bounds, that is, beyond
the recognized boundaries of a golf course as determined by
white stakes, another ball must be played from where that original shot was taken, adding one stroke to the score. In other words,
it is stroke-and-distance; generally it's a tee-shot, so you go back
to the tee and hit three. The same rule applies to a lost ball.

The argument against the rule is the part about having to go
back to where you hit the ball that went out of bounds. The distance thing. Walter Hagen made the point, in the 1930s, that a
golfer may hit a ball into a water hazard 150 yards off the tee,
say, and play another ball at the point where the ball entered the
water, taking the one-shot penalty. Whereas, a golfer may hit a
250-yard drive that is out of bounds by a mere inch—in other
words, a much better shot than that which went into the water—
but must give up that distance. Why not simply play your third
shot from the point where your ball went out of bounds, and play
three from there? Just as is done with a ball in a water hazard.
Good point, and it was made many times over the years. In 1950
the R&A made it a stroke-only penalty, wherein you could play
your third shot from the point where the ball went out of bounds.
The USGA tried that in 1952. Both went back to stroke-and-distance, for no clear reason. It might have had something to do with
the determination of just where the ball went out of bounds—on
what line—and players taking advantage in the determination
to have a better third-shot position. However, that judgment is
made as a matter of course when a ball is hit into the water that is
a lateral hazard. So why can't it be for an out-of-bounds ball? In
1960 the USGA tried a distance-only regulation—you went back
to the tee and hit two, not three. But it rescinded that rule the next
year, again without a clear reason.

First City-Owned Public (or Muni, for Municipal) Golf Course in the United States, **Van Cortlandt Park GC, New York City.** It opened in 1895, and is still in use.

First City-Owned Public Golf Course in the United States to Charge a Greens Fee, **Jackson Park GC, Chicago.** Opened in 1899, it was the first public course west of the Alleghenies Mountains. It is still in play. The first greens fee, initiated because so many players were using the course, was 10 cents per round.

First Private Golf Club in the United States, **St. Andrews Golf Club, Yonkers, New York,** 1888. Conventional wisdom has it that St. Andrews is also the birthplace of American golf, but in fact the game was played in America well before the above date on courses around Savannah, Georgia, Charleston, South Carolina, West Virginia, and Pennsylvania.

First Private Golf Club Membership Waiting List, **Shinnecock Hills GC, West Hampton, NY.**

First American President to Take Up Golf, **William Howard Taft,** who held the office from 1909 through 1913. Theodore Roosevelt, who preceded Taft in the White House, remarked to Taft in no uncertain terms that he should not play the game because it was undemocratic, and also because it was a "sissy" game and for that reason alone should be ignored. Better to shoot beautiful animals with a powerful gun, thought TR. Taft ignored the "Rough Rider," as did a number of presidents to follow.

First Designer of a Golf Course, **Allan Robertson,** a Scot who is also regarded as the

First Golf Professional. In 1848, Robertson made modifications on the Old Course (St. Andrews), creating the double greens, widening the fairways, and designing from scratch the famous (in my mind infamous) 17th hole—the Road Hole. He also laid out links courses in various districts of Scotland, including a ten-hole layout in Barry, Angus, Scotland, that became Carnoustie GC. Robertson was by all accounts the *First Greenskeeper.* (Now referred to as a course maintenance supervisor.)

First Golf Clubhouse in the United States, **Shinnecock Hills GC, on Long Island, New York.** It was designed by the famous American architect, Stanford White, in 1891, and exists to this day on the site of the club.

First Time Professionals Allowed into Clubhouse, **1914.** Traditional history has had it that this occurred in 1920 at the Inverness Club in Toledo, when the US Open was being played there, and that Walter Hagen led the charge. However, Herb Graffis, the pioneer American golf writer, historian of the PGA of America, and publisher had a different take. Graffis noted that in the days leading up to the 1914 US Open, at the Midlothian CC, outside Chicago, the members of the club wondered where the pros would hang their coats. They had always used nails on a wall in the back of the pro shop, but there were not enough nails to accommodate the large number of pros who would be in the field. A member of the club suggested room could be made in the clubhouse. When other members claimed the pros were not gentlemen, the maverick member replied that the club's own professional, George Turnbull, was one of the finest gentlemen in the world. Everyone agreed, and the pros were allowed in the clubhouse. Apparently, Graffis concluded, because Hagen was the first pro to walk into the clubhouse he received credit for the breakthrough, or breakdown of a social prejudice. That he won the championship also helped.

First Nassau Competition, **1901 (approximately).** According to Findlay Douglas, the 1898 US Amateur champion, players in interclub team matches held in the New York area did not enjoy seeing newspaper accounts of their being beaten badly—like nine and eight. So one day when the matches were held at the Nassau CC in Glen Cove (on Long Island), New York, the host team devised a scoring system whereby one point went to the winner of each nine holes and one for the entire eighteen. Thus, no one could lose by more than three points. Face was saved, at least in the public prints, and golf eventually had its most popular betting game.

First Time a Fee Was Charged to Play St. Andrews Old, **1913,** when the course was seven hundred years old. The 1894 Act of Parliament allowed for the R&A to charge visiting golfers playing the New Course during the months of July, August, and September. The 1913 Act empowered the town council of St. Andrews to charge people playing the Old Course, but not municipal voters, members of the R&A, or members of the Cheape family (the owners of the Strathyrum Estate and guests. Could this be where the word *cheap* arose into the language?). It also had the power to reduce the charges for students of the university and members of local golf clubs who were not permanently resident in St. Andrews. The cost in all these instances is lost in the mists of time. When I played the Old Course the first time, in 1964, it cost £1, which was $2.80. Today the price is £140 (High Season: April 18 through October 16), £91 (Shoulder Season: April 4 through 17), and £64 (Low Season: January 1 through March 3).

First Golf Resort, **Biarritz, France.** In 1888 some wealthy Britons who were into golf built a course in Biarritz so they could keep up their game during the winter months. Biarritz is in the southwest corner of France, eighteen miles from the Spanish border, and has mild winters compared to those in England. Arnaud Massy, the first French golf champion, was born and raised in Biarritz.

First Hole-in-One in a Major Competition, "Young" Tom Morris, in the 1868 British Open. He holed out on the 8th at Prestwick. It helped him to the first of four consecutive victories in the championship, all at Prestwick.

First Time Golf Included in the Olympic Games, 1900. At the Games in Paris, American and French women played a nine-hole tournament that was won by Margaret Ives Abbott, an American, who shot a 47. She never knew the tournament was part of the Olympics, or that she was **The First Female American Olympic Champion.** She did not receive a medal, gold or otherwise. They were doing trophies then, and apparently they were not inscribed with any Olympic Games designation.

In that same Olympics men competed on a somewhat more substantial level. An American, Charles Sands, shot rounds of 82–85 to win the gold by two strokes. Sands noted afterward that tennis was his best game.

Golf was included in the 1904 Olympics, but only for men. Seventy-five entered and tried to qualify for a field of thirty-two contestants. All were either American or Canadian. In the final, George Lyon of Canada defeated Chandler Egan of America, three and two. Play was at the Glen Echo GC in St. Louis, which was built in 1901 and is considered **The First Eighteen-Hole Golf Course in the United States Built West of the Mississippi River.**

Golf was never included in the Olympic Games afterward, but it will be included starting in 2016 and will be played by professionals.

First Cross-Handed Golfer to Compete Nationally, Howard Wheeler, a lanky African American professional from the Philadelphia area. He was one of the best players ever on the Negro Tour in the years before the end of racial segregation on the PGA Tour. He was an exceptionally long hitter off the tee, once driving the green of the 335-yard 17th hole at Tam O'Shanter CC during the All-American tournament. He was among the first African Americans invited to compete against white players. Wheeler also had a peculiar way of teeing up his ball, propping it on a matchbook cover he formed into a cylinder.

First Left-Hander to Win the NCAA Individual, US Amateur, US Open, and Masters, **Phil Mickelson**.

First Left-Handed Golfers Association, **1932.** Babe Ruth was the first president.

First Natural Left-Hander Who Could Have Been Far More Successful if He Had Been Allowed to Play as a Lefty, **Johnny Bulla.** Bulla grew up at a time when it was still thought that doing anything left handed was the work of the devil. Fortunately, Bulla was ambidextrous enough to make the switch to the right side and have a pretty decent career. He had two seconds in the British Open, won the Los Angeles Open, and contended closely in the US Open. However, he was convinced that had he been allowed to play left-handed he would have been a world-beater.

First Golf Shot Hit on the Moon, **February 9, 1971.** On that date the Apollo 14 Moon Mission landed on the distant planet, and astronaut Alan Shepard took a few moments from his assigned tasks to hit a shot with a rigged-up Wilson Dyna-Power "Button-Back" 6-iron he sneaked aboard. He hit two shots, with only one arm, and they presumably, or the science says, are still going, which makes them the longest golf shots ever hit.

First Canadian Open Champion, **J. H. Oke,** 1904. It is golf's third-oldest national championship, and third oldest on the PGA Tour after the US and Western Opens.

First Handicapped Golfers Association of America National Champion, **J. B. Bass,** 1933.

First National Golf Exhibition and Merchandise Show, **1926,** in Chicago.

Golfdom's Most Popular Clubhouse/Locker Room/Grill Room Card Game, **gin rummy.**

Most Penalty Strokes Assessed in One Round, **Eighteen,** to Paul Farmer, in the 1960 Texas Open. He changed putters after the front nine and was assessed two strokes per hole, or the entire back nine. It gave him a round of 88.

First Person to Create a Yardage Book, **Gene Andrews,** in the 1950s. Andrews, a fine California amateur golfer, was also a methodical, "scientific" player. He began making notes recording the yardages from tees to fairway bunkers, from various parts of the fairway and rough to the greens, undulations and the like and referred to them during tournament rounds. Deane Beman, a nationally ranked amateur, a pro tour player, and eventually the commissioner of the PGA Tour, had played some amateur golf with Andrews and picked up on his yardage book idea. He told it to his pal, Jack Nicklaus, who liked the idea and began doing it himself. Being Jack Nicklaus, the idea was popularized, and it is now a common tool among tournament players.

Jack Fleck, the 1955 US Open champion, claims to have come before Andrews in creating a yardage book, but no one recalls seeing him use one in play.

First Golf Comic Strip, **Mac Divot.** Mel Keefer and Jordan Lansky created it. Other comic strips had the occasional single strip with a golf theme, but Mac Divot was devoted entirely to the game. It ran for some two decades, from the 1950s into the 1970s, originating in the *Chicago Tribune.*

First Ticker-Tape Parade for a Golfer, **1930,** for Bobby Jones, after he won the British Open and British Amateur championships. It was up Broadway, in New York City. Ben Hogan would be the next golfer to be so feted when he won the 1953 British Open.

First Movie Star with an Uncle Who Was a Golf Champion, **Jon Voight.** Jon Voight's father, Elmer, was a golf professional whose promise as a player was dashed by a serious injury. He became a highly regarded golf teacher. Elmer's brother, George Voight, was a fine amateur in the 1920s. He won three straight North-South Amateurs, played Walker Cup golf, and went to the semis in the 1928 US Amateur. He then became an East Coast club professional. Jon Voight's most famous movie roles were in *Midnight Cowboy* and *Deliverance.* There is no record of him playing much golf, if at all.

First Notable American Amateur Golfer to Sire a Hall-of-Fame Baseball Player, **Charlie Seaver,** who won numerous California amateur championships, played Walker Cup golf, was a medalist in one US Amateur and semifinalist in 1903. He lost to Eugene Homans in that semi. If he had won, he would have played Bobby Jones for the title. Many thought if it was Seaver Jones had to play he might not have completed his Grand Slam. Seaver was that good. His son, **Tom Seaver,** became one of major league baseball's best-ever pitchers and a member of the baseball Hall of Fame.

First Sudden-Death Playoff to Win a Major, **1977,** when Lanny Wadkins defeated Gene Littler on the third extra hole of the PGA Championship, at Pebble Beach Golf Links. Wadkins holed a 6-foot putt for a par to clinch the title.

First to Win Three Majors in One Year, **Ben Hogan,** in 1953, when he won the Masters, US Open and British Open. Call it the Tri-Slam. Hogan did not try for the PGA championship that year to complete the modern Grand Slam because of conflicting dates—the day before Hogan teed off in the first round of the British Open the final match of the PGA championship was being played. Furthermore, Hogan was no longer entering the PGA championship, then at match play, because it would require far more golf than his battered legs could withstand.

First Practice Range, **1920,** at the storied Pinehurst Golf Resort, in North Carolina. It was, and still is, called "Maniac Hill."

First Winner of the Four Modern Majors a Second Time, **Jack Nicklaus,** when he won the 1971 PGA Championship.

FIRST STATE OPEN CHAMPIONS (MEN)

Alabama, **Hack Lowery,** 1937. Notable Others: Gardner Dickinson (match play), Harold Williams, Jon Gustin, Steve Lowery.

Alaska, **Rick Larson,** 1980.

Arizona, **Johnny Bulla,** 1958. Notable Others: Al Mengert, Kermit Zarley, Dale Douglass, Steve Spray.

Arkansas, **E. J. "Dutch" Harrison,** 1937. Notable Others: Gib Sellers, Buster Cupit, Al Mengert, and Chuck Thorpe.

California, **Fred Morrison,** 1937. Notable Others: George Von Elm, Art Bell, Olin Dutra, John Dawson (A), George Fazio, Smiley Quick, E. J. "Dutch" Harrison, Zell Eaton, Lloyd Mangrum, Eric Monti, Jerry Barber, Bud Holscher, Steve Opperman, Roger Maltbie, Rex Caldwell, Greg Twiggs.

Colorado, **John E. Rogers,** 1948. Notable Others: Orville Moody, Bill Bisdorf, Dave Hill, Larry Mowry, Dan Halldorson, Willie Wood, Al Geiberger, Mark Wiebe, Steve Jones.

Connecticut, **Henry Ciuci,** 1931. Notable Others: John Golden, Harry Cooper, Jimmy Demaret, Ted Lenczyk (A), Dick Siderowf (A), Ken Green.

Delaware, **Clint Kennedy,** 1966.

Florida, **Lou Broward,** 1942. Notable Others: Willie Turnesa (A), Pete Cooper, Gardner Dickinson, Howell Fraser (A), Don Bisplinghoff (A), J. C. Goosie, Bob Murphy (A), Gary Koch (A), Eddie Pearce (A), Ted Kroll, Billy Maxwell, Larry Mowry, Bruce Fleisher, Donnie Hammond, John Huston, Bart Bryant, Dave Ragan, Jim King.

Georgia, **Jim Stamps,** 1958. Notable Others: Tommy Aaron (A), Steve Melnyk (A), Lynn Lott (A), Hugh Royer, DeWitt Weaver, Larry Nelson, Bob Tway, Tim Simpson, Gene Sauers.

Hawaii, **Gay Brewer,** 1965. Notable Others: A longtime PGA Tour stop going back to the 1920s, it has had many celebrated winners. Some include: Ted Makalena (the *First Native Hawaiian to Win a PGA Tour Event*), Dudley Wysong, Bruce Crampton, Grier Jones, Wayne Levi, Hale Irwin, Lee Trevino, Jack Nicklaus, Ben Crenshaw, Hubert Green, Corey Pavin, Lanny Wadkins, John Cook, Paul Azinger, Ernie Els, V. J. Singh, and Jim Furyk.

Idaho, **Tony Lema,** 1958. Notable Others: Smiley Quick, Al Mengert.

Illinois, **Abe Espinosa,** 1931. Notable Others: James Foulis Sr., Harry Cooper, Zell Eaton, Dick Metz, Felice Torza, Bill Ogden, Errie Ball, Jock Hutchison Jr., Jack Fleck, Chick Evans (A), Gary Hallberg (A), David Ogrin.

Indiana, **Sidney Cooper*,** 1915. Notable Others: Cyril Walker, Bob Hamilton, Fred Wampler (A), Dale Morey (A), Joe Campbell

(A), Bill Kratzert (A), Wally Armstrong, Jim Gallagher. *Sidney Cooper was the father of Harry Cooper, one of the best tour players in the game in the 1930s.

Iowa, **Denmar Miller**, 1933. Notable Others: Harold "Jug" McSpaden, Johnny Dawson (A), Leonard Dodson, Herman Keiser, Labron Harris, Wally Ulrich, Bob Stone, Steve Spray, Eddie Langert.

Kansas, **Phil Rodgers**, 1976. Notable Others: Gary McCord, Stan Utley.

Kentucky, **Bob Craigs**, 1920. Notable Others: Craig Wood, Byron Nelson, Gay Brewer, Frank Beard, and Jodie Mudd.

Louisiana, **Frank Champ**, 1947. Notable Others: Homero Blancas, Sammy Rachels.

Maine, **A. H. Fenn**, 1918. Notable Others: Bob Toski, Bill Ezinicki.

Maryland, **D. Clarke Corkran**, 1921. Notable Others: Wiffy Cox, Leo Diegel, Fred McLeod, Bobby Cruickshank, Vic Ghezzi, Lew Worsham, Jack Isaacs, Charles Bassler, Deane Beman (A), Fred Funk.

Massachusetts, **Donald Ross**, 1905. Notable Others: Alex Ross, Tom McNamara, Mike Brady, Walter Hagen, Jesse Guilford (A), Willie Ogg, Johnny Farrell, Leo Diegel, Joe Turnesa, Francis Ouimet (A), Gene Kunes, Julius Boros, Ed "Porky" Oliver, Bob Toski, Bill Ezinicki, Paul Harney (A), Jay Dolan, Bob Menne, Dana Quigley, Jim Hallet.

Michigan, **Dave Robertson**, 1925. Notable Others: Al Watrous, George Von Elm, Charles Kocsis (A), Mortie Dutra, Melvin "Chick" Harbert, Gib Sellers, Sam Byrd, O'Neal "Buck" White, Walter Burkemo, Pete Cooper, John Barnum, Dave Hill, Pete Brown, Mike Souchak, George Bayer.

Minnesota, **Tom Stevens**, 1917. Notable Others: George Sargent, Jack Burke Sr., Jimmy Johnston, Lester Bolstad, Harry Cooper, Wally Ulrich, Joel Goldstrand, Don Croonquist, Jon Chaffee, Tom Lehman.

Mississippi, **Harry Walker**, 1927. Notable Others: E. J. "Dutch" Harrison, Johnny Revolta, Fred Haas Jr.

Missouri, **Bob Stone**, 1975. Notable Others: Jay Haas, Joe Jimenez, Bobby Stroble, Phil Blackmar, Stan Utley.

Montana, **Smiley Quick**, 1958. Notable Others: E. J. "Dutch" Harrison, Bob Duden.

Nebraska, **Mark Rohde**, 1979.

Nevada, **Bob Hamilton**, 1946. Notable Others: E. J. "Dutch" Harrison, George Schneiter, Joe Porter, Larry Mowry, Willie Wood, Kirk Triplett.

New Hampshire, **Gene Mosher**, 1932. Notable Others: Tony Manero, Frank Walsh, Bill Ezinicki, Wayne Levi, Frank Fuhrer III.

New Jersey, **Peter O'Hara**, 1921. Notable Others: Johnny Golden, Paul Runyan, Craig Wood, Byron Nelson, Johnny Farrell, Vic Ghezzi, Jim Barnes, Al Mengert.

New Mexico, **Harry Loudermilk**, 1958.

New York, **Bill Springer**, 1977. Notable Others: George Burns, Joey Sindelar, and Lon Nielsen.

North Dakota, **Jack Webb**, 1965.

Ohio, **Emmett French**, 1924. Notable Others: Denny Shute (A), Al Espinosa, Billy Burke, Byron Nelson, Frank Stranahan (A), Herman Keiser, Jack Nicklaus (A), Bob Shave Jr., Tom Weiskopf, Bob Wynn.

Oklahoma, **William Nichols**, 1910. Notable Others: Bill Mehlhorn, Ed Dudley, Dick Grout, Harold "Jug" McSpaden, Walter Emery (A), Zell Eaton, Chuck Klein, Labron Harris Jr., Buster Cupit, Babe Hiskey, Bob Dickson, Grier Jones, Bobby Stroble, Danny Edwards, Mark Hayes, Lindy Miller, Gil Morgan, Doug Tewell, Bob Tway.

Oregon, **George Smith**, 1905. Notable Others: Tommy Armour, Horton Smith, Gene Sarazen, Ray Mangrum, Al Zimmerman, Bob Duden, Chuck Congdon, Peter Jacobsen (A), Bruce Cudd, Rick Acton, Pat Fitzsimons.

Pennsylvania, **Tom Anderson**, 1912. Notable Others: MacDonald Smith, Jock Hutchison, Dick Metz, Willie MacFarlane, Ray Mangrum, Toney Penna, Lloyd Mangrum, Sam Parks, Sam Byrd, Jerry Barber, Johnny Bulla, Bob Winninger, Henry Williams, Skee Riegel, Al Besselink, Jay Sigel (A).

Rhode Island, **Fred Bentley**, 1929. Notable Others: Jim Turnesa, Johnny Farrell, and Bill Ezinicki.

South Dakota, **Eddie McElligott**, 1934.

Tennessee, **Pat Abbott**, 1949. Notable Others: Curtis Person (A), Mason Rudolph (A), Joe Campbell, J. C. Goosie, Larry Gilbert, Gibby Gilbert, Bobby Nichols, Loren Roberts.

Texas, **Bob McDonald**, 1922. Notable Others: Just about anybody who was anybody, as it was a regular PGA Tour stop. But to name a few: Walter Hagen, Joe Turnesa, MacDonald Smith, E. J. "Dutch" Harrison, Bill Mehlhorn, Byron Nelson, Lawson Little, Sam Byrd, Ben Hogan, Sam Snead, Jack Burke Jr., Gene Littler, Mike Souchak, Arnold Palmer, Lee Trevino, Ben Crenshaw.

Utah, **Eddie Morrison**, 1926. Notable Others: Ky Laffoon, Fred Morrison, George Schneiter, Al Zimmerman, Ed Dudley, Harold

"Jug" McSpaden, Johnny Palmer, Lloyd Mangrum, Zell Eaton, Ellsworth Vines, Dow Finsterwald, Bob Rosburg, Al Geiberger, Tommy Jacobs, Victor Regalado, Randy Glover, Gary Vanier, Mike Reid, Richard Zokol, Jay Don Blake.

Vermont, **John Thoren**, 1949. Notable Others: Jay Dolan, Bill Ezinicki, Les Kennedy, Lance Ten Broeck, Dana Quigley.

Virginia, **Al Smith**, 1958. Notable Others: Chandler Harper, Bobby Mitchell, Tom Strange (father of Curtis), Vinny Giles (A), Lanny Wadkins, Robert Wrenn, Mark Carnevale.

Washington, **Al Espinosa**, 1923. Notable Others: Marvin "Bud" Ward, Charles Congdon, Don Bies, Al Mengert, Ken Still, Dave Barr, Fred Couples.

West Virginia, **Johnny Javins**, 1933. Notable Others: Sam Snead, Bill Campbell (A), Ed Tutwiler (A).

Wisconsin, **W. R. Lovekin**, 1919. Notable Others: Frank Walsh, Johnny Revolta, Manuel de la Torre, Bobby Brue, Tommy Veech (A), Dennis Tiziani, Steve Stricker, Skip Kendall.

Wyoming, **Merle Bachland**, 1958. Notable Others: Dale Douglass, Bill Bisdorf.

 FIRST STATE AMATEUR CHAMPIONS (MEN AND WOMEN)

State:	Men:	Women:
Alabama	**Hack Lowery** (1937)	**Mrs. Sam Upchurch** (1963)

Notable Others: Gardner Dickinson, Hubert Green, B. R. MacLendon, Steve Lowery, Sam Farlow

Alaska	**Orville Smith** (1958)	**Electra Joiner** (1958)

Arizona	**H. S. Corbett**	**Mrs. J. M. Williams**
	(1923)	**(1933)**

Notable Others: Bob Goldwater, Heather Farr, Ed Updegraff, Joe Porter, Tom Purtzer

Arkansas	**J. E. England**	**Mrs. Carle Robbins**
	(1916)	**(1935)**

Notable Other: Labron Harris

California	**J. F. Neville (1912)**	**Mrs. Luther Kennett**
		(1920)

Notable Others: Charles Seaver, Beverly Hanson, Barbara Romack, Ken Venturi, Gene Littler, Forest Fezler, Patty Sheehan, John Cook, Bobby Clampett, Mark O'Meara, Duffy Waldorf, Kris Moe, Charlie Wi, Jason Gore, Spencer Levin

Colorado	**Frank Woodward**	**Mrs. Burnside**
	(1901)	**Winslow (1919)**

Notable Others: Lawson Little, John Dawson, Hale Irwin, Steve Ziegler

Connecticut	**C. C. Clare (1931)**	**Mrs. M. A.**
		McLaughlin
		(1916)

Notable Others: Dick Siderowf, Ted Lencyzk

Delaware	**Ellis Taylor (1949)**	

Florida	**A. C. Ulmer (1914)**	**Mrs. John Holmes**
		(1927)

Notable Others: Don Bisplinghoff, Mrs. Alice Dye, Frank Strafaci, Bob Murphy, Gary Koch, Jerry Pate, Bob Murphy, David Peoples, Lee Rinker

Georgia	**R. T. "Bobby" Jones**	**Mrs. W. D. Doak**
	Jr. (1916)	**(1930)**

Notable Others: Perry Adair, Watts Gunn, Louise Suggs, Mary Lena, Charles Yates, E. Harvie Ward, Tommy Aaron, Hollis Stacy, Allen Doyle, Danny Yates

| Hawaii | Owen Douglass (1963) | Joan Damon (1963) |

Notable Other: David Ishii

| Idaho | Warren Dawson (1931) | Mrs. Phil Ashforth (1934) |

| Illinois | H. I. Miller (1900) | Dorothy Foster (1934) |

Notable Others: Gary Hallberg, David Ogrin

| Indiana | H. I. Miller (1900) | Mrs. B. C. Stevenson (1922) |

Notable Others: Bob Hamilton, Dale Morey, Alice O'Neal/Alice Dye, Fred Wampler, Pete Dye, Sam Carmichael, Ed Tutwiler, Joe Campbell, Bill Kratzert, Fuzzy Zoeller

| Iowa | Dr. John Maxwell (1900) | Lucille Robinson (1933) |

Notable Others: Jack Rule, Steve Spray, Lon Nielsen

| Kansas | Paul Hyde (1908) | Sally Sterriett (1919) |

Notable Others: Jim Colbert, Grier Jones

| Kentucky | I. F. Starks (1911) | Mrs. Chas. McGraw (1923) |

Notable Others: Gay Brewer, Bobby Nichols, Frank Beard, Jodie Mudd, Steve Flesch

| Louisiana | J. K. Whadley (1920) | Mrs. Ruth Reymond (1926) |

Notable Other: Fred Haas Jr.

| Maine | W. P. Hersey (1923) | Helen Payson (1921) |

| Maryland | B. Warren Corkran (1921) | Mrs. Joan Greiner (1921) |

Notable Others: Otto Greiner, Ralph Bogart, Martin West

| Massachusetts | Arthur Lockwood (1903) | Grace Keyes (1900) |

Notable Others: Francis Ouimet, Jesse Guilford, Margaret
Curtis, Glen Collett, Ed Lowery, Ted Bishop, Robert
Knowles, Dorothy Hurd

| Michigan | Jas. T. Wylie (1906) | Mrs. John Case (1914) |

Notable Other: Chuck Kocsis

| Minnesota | T. P. Thurston (1901) | Mrs. Dansingburg (1939) |
| Mississippi | W. E. Ware (1915) | Mrs. Ben Fitzhugh (1930) |

Notable Others: Curtis Person, Eddie Merrins

| Missouri | H. W. Allen (1905) | Grace Semple (1915) |

Notable Others: Jim Colbert, Tom Watson, Payne Stewart

| Montana | E. J. Parker (1917) | Mrs. I. M. Wheeler (1917) |

| Nebraska | E. P. Boyer (1905) | Louise Pond (1916) |

Notable Other: Johnny Goodman.

| Nevada | Wayne Adams Jr. (1947) | Mrs. Fred Apostoli (1942) |

Notable Other: Robert Gamez

| New Hampshire | Nat Hobbs (1906) | Katherine Sheehan (1938) |

| New Jersey | Archibald Graham (1900) | Mrs. Thomas Hacknall (1923) |

Notable Others: Jerry Travers, Max Marston, Maureen Orcutt,
Walt Zembriski, Chet Sanok, Bob Housen

| New Mexico | H. Iverson (1915) | Elinor Jones (1934) |

Notable Others: Nancy Lopez, Kathy Whitworth, Rosie Jones

| New York | Edmond Driggs Jr. (1923) | Helen Hicks (1930) |

Notable Others: Ray Billows, Dick Chapman, Willie Turnesa, Sam Urzetta, Dick Mayer, Terry Diehl, Jeff Sluman, Joey Sindelar

North Carolina   **Bill Dean (1958)**   **Marge Burns (1958)**
Notable Others: Dale Morey, Joe Inman, Scott Hoch, Vance Heafner

North Dakota   **John Reuter (1919)**   **Mrs. Roy Hall (1928)**

Ohio   **T. Sterling Beckwith (1904)**   **Katherine Starbuck (1920)**
Notable Others: Denny Shute, Frank Stranahan, Peggy Kirk (Bell), Arnold Palmer, John Cook

Oklahoma   **Harry Gwinnup (1910)**   **Mrs. Arthur Will (1915)**
Notable Others: Bo Winninger, Labron Harris Jr., Bob Dickson, Mark Hayes, Dave Barr, Lucas Glover, Willie Wood, Todd Hamilton, David Edwards

Oregon   **R. L. MacLeay (1904)**   **Carrie Flanders (1904)**
Notable Others: Dick Yost, Don Moe, Bruce Cudd

Pennsylvania   **Harold B. McFarland (1909)**   **Francis Williams (1933)**
Notable Others: W. C. Fownes, Max Marston, Helen Sigel, Carol Semple, Jay Sigel, Jim Simons

Rhode Island   **Eden Byers (1902)**   **Elizabeth Gordon (1916)**
Notable Other: Billy Andrade

South Carolina   **Emory Harper (1949)**   **Mrs. H. S. Covington (1949)**

| South Dakota | Ed Meisenholder (1921) | Mrs. O. C. Ellison (1925) |

Notable Other: Alice Bauer

| Tennessee | Bradley Waler (1914) | Mrs. David Gaut (1937) |

Notable Others: Cary Middlecoff, Hillman Robbins, Lew Oehmig

| Texas | H. L. Edwards (1906) | Edna Lapham (1916) |

Notable Others: Gus Moreland, Earl Stewart Jr., Betty Jameson, Betsy Rawls, Ernie Vossler, Don Massengale, Charles Coody, Sandra Haynie, Sandra Palmer, Marty Fleckman, Bruce Lietzke, Ben Crenshaw, Mark Brooks, Scott Verplank

| Utah | R. B. Harkness (1899) | Mrs. A. H. Means (1932) |

Notable Other: George Von Elm

| Vermont | Paul Waterman (1902) | Mrs. Fred Davis (1930) |

| Virginia | William H. Palmer Jr. (1911) | Mrs. J. W. Zimmerman (1922) |

Notable Others: Chandler Harper, Vinny Giles, Lanny Wadkins, Curtis Strange

| Washington | Bon Stein (1922) | Mrs. I. S. Patterson (1922) |

Notable Others: Al Mengert, Kermit Zarley

| West Virginia | Julius Pollock Jr. (1916) | Mrs. E. C. Dawley (1916) |

Notable Others: Denny Shute, Ed Tutwiler, Bill Campbell

| Wisconsin | Hamilton Vose (1901) | Francis Hadfield (1917) |

Notable Others: Lyn Lardner, Wilf Wehrle, Bob Brue, Andy North

| Wyoming | Maj. H. C. Dagley
(1923) | Mrs. Art Forbes
(1933) |

 **MOSTS**

Most Condescending Remark Made After a Player Hits a Marginally Decent Shot, "That'll play." Or, a variant: "That'll work."

Most Successful Professional Entertainer/Golfer, **Don Cherry.** A highly popular and successful popular singer (crooner) who played all the top nightclubs in the country and was a regular on Dean Martin's television shows. He played on three US Walker Cup teams, in nine Masters, eight US Opens, and had a chance to win the 1960 US Open with nine holes to play; he finished second low amateur to Jack Nicklaus.

Most Dramatic Golf Shot Ever Hit before the Smallest Audience, **Gene Sarazen's** second shot with a 4-wood on the 15th (69th) hole of the 1935 Masters. Although over the years Sarazen was told by thousands of people that they saw the shot, Sarazen said about six or seven people were "in the house" in the late afternoon of the fourth round when it happened. Frank Walsh, a well-known professional of the time, was on hand and remembered that two spectators were at the green and were going onto it as though to take the ball out of the hole. "I remember Gene shouting at them," said Walsh, 'Get the hell away from there,' or words to that effect." Walter Hagen was paired with Sarazen, but apparently he didn't see the shot. He was "way over on the other side of the fairway playing short of the green," according to Walsh. Hagen never did mention the shot in the years to come, perhaps because the younger Sarazen had become his chief rival. Or simply because he didn't see it.

Most Dramatic Golf Shot Ever Hit before the Largest Audience, **Larry Mize's** pitch-and-run hole-out on the 11th hole at Augusta

National to win the 1987 Masters in a sudden-death playoff with Greg Norman (Seve Ballesteros bowed out on the 10th hole with a bogey). Seen by many millions around the world on television.

Most Professional Major Victories, **Eighteen,** by Jack Nicklaus. They include: The US Open (four), the Masters (five), the PGA Championship (five), the British Open (four).

Most Second-Place Finishes in Majors, **Nineteen,** Jack Nicklaus. He finished either sole second or tied four times in the US Open, seven times in the British Open, four times in the Masters, and four times in the PGA championship.

Most Money Won in a Calcutta Pool, **$72,900,** to Frankie Laine, the popular singer of the 1950s, who bought Gene Littler to win the 1953 Tournament of Champions. It was played, of course, in Las Vegas.

Most Frequently Asked and Never Answered Question in Golf, **"How did that ball stay out of the hole?"** Or, **"How did that ball not go in?"** Invariably they reference a putt.

Oldest Continuously Operating Golf Club in North America, **Royal Montreal GC,** in Canada, which was established in 1873.

Longest Last Name to Win a Major Title, **Mark Calcavecchia,** 1989 British Open.

Laurie Auchterlonie, 1893 British Open (twelve letters, one more than Ballesteros).

Longest Golf Course in the World, **International GC,** in Bolton, Massachusetts. It plays 8,325 yards from the tips. Par is 77.

Longest Drive Hit in Competition, **515 Yards,** by Mike Austin, an original member of the 350-Club (a Long-Drive Group). In the 1974 US National Senior championship in Las Vegas, played at the Winterwood GC, Austin used a thirty-five mph tail wind on the 450-yard 5th hole and played a sixty-five-yard second shot back into the wind with a hard 9-iron.

Most Consecutive Aces in Competition, **Two,** by Bob Hudson, in the 1971 Martini International, Norwich, England. In his second round he aced the 11th and 12th holes.

Most Holes-in-One by Individual, **Fifty-one,** by Mancil Davis, a pro who played a bit on the pro tour.

Longest Hole-in-One, **517 yards,** by Mike Crean on the 16th hole at Green Valley Ranch GC, in Denver. He had some help from the altitude, but still.

Oldest Ace Maker, **Harold Stilson,** a 101-year old Floridian who did the deed on the 108-yard 16th at the Deerfield CC, Deerfield Beach, Florida. It was his sixth, overall.

Most Often Broken Rule, **Failure to Hole Out Every Putt.**

Most National Championships Won in Same Year, **Three,** the 1971 US and British Opens and the Canadian Open, Lee Trevino.

Most Number of Outstanding Courses within the Smallest Area, **Four,** The Olympic CC, Lake Merced GC, San Francisco GC, and Harding Park GC, all within a five-mile radius on the far west side of San Francisco. The Olympic Club has hosted five US Opens to date; Lake Merced is one of golf's best-kept secrets; San Francisco GC is the je ne sais quoi of golf; Harding Park, the only public course in the bunch, was for many years the site of a regular PGA Tour event, and more recently the President's Cup and the Schwab Cup, a senior tour event.

Most Compelling Round of Competitive Golf, **Final Round of the 1977 British Open,** at Turnberry GC. Jack Nicklaus and Tom Watson traded birdies throughout the round, with Watson outlasting Nicklaus 65 to 66 to take the title.

Most Consecutive Years with at Least One Victory, **Seventeen,** Arnold Palmer and Jack Nicklaus.

Most Frequently Played Public Golf Course, **Rancho Park GC,** in Los Angeles, California, with an average of 120,000 rounds per year.

Most Expensive Green Fee at a "Public" Course, **$450** (so far) for eighteen holes at Pebble Beach Golf Links, with no rain check or a extra few holes if there is still some light. And you can't take your cart into the fairways. What's more, a walk-on round is almost impossible. Your best chance to get on is if you stay at The Lodge, a very pricey hotel a short walk from the first tee. For all that, it's booked solid almost all year. And is classified as a public course.

Highest Course in the World, **La Paz GC, Bolivia,** at 10,650 feet.

Highest Course in the United States, **Copper Creek GC,** Colorado, at 9,700 feet.

Coldest Golf Course in the World, **North Star GC,** in Alaska.

Hottest Golf Course in the World, **Alice Springs GC,** Australia.

Lowest Golf Course in the World, **Furnace Creek GC,** California, at 214 feet below sea level.

Northernmost Golf Course in the World, **North Cape GC, Norway** (six holes).

Southernmost Golf Course in the World, **Ushuara GC, Argentina,** 55 degrees latitude.

Most Bunkered Course in the World, **Whistling Straits GC, Kohler, Wisconsin,** with anywhere from 900 to 1,200. Even the owners of the course, and the architect, Pete Dye, don't know exactly how many. Quite a few of the bunkers are not in unconventional locations, which created an unfortunate episode in the 2010 PGA Championship. Dustin Johnson, on the 18th hole, and the 72nd of the tournament, needed a par-4 to win the title. However, his drive went to the far right and finished in a bunker. Trouble was, he didn't recognize it as such, perhaps because it was so far right and some people in the gallery had trampled through it during the day. In fact, a few were standing in the right edge when Johnson reached his ball, and Johnson assumed he was not in the bunker but only on a random patch of sandy soil. Therefore, he grounded his club behind the ball when playing his shot, with a long iron, which came up short of the green. After pitching onto the putting surface, he two putted for a bogey and ended up in a tie with Martin Kraymer and Bubba Watson.

However, it was duly noted and reported that Johnson had grounded his club in the bunker, and upon review of the television footage PGA officials, and Johnson himself, agreed that he was in a bunker and in grounding and his club should be assessed a two-stroke penalty. He was now out of the playoff (which Kraymer won), finishing in a tie for third. Johnson could blame no one but himself. The PGA of America, which conducts the championship, made it very clear in its local rules passed out to all players and posted in convenient locations around the locker room that these outlying bunkers were indeed bunkers. Johnson said afterward that he never read the instruction sheet.

Most Consecutive Victories in a Tournament, **Four,** Walter Hagen, PGA Championship (1924, 1927), Tiger Woods, Bay Hill Invitational (2000, 2003) and Buick Invitational (2005, 2008).

Most Common Golf Dream. Research I've done on golf dreams indicates that the most common one is a situation where you are unable to make a backswing because you have immediately behind you an immovable obstacle such as a wall or thick bushes or are in a very small space such as a phone booth or tiny room. If you can't get the club back, you can't hit the shot. Obviously. A second common dream (almost all golf dreams involve difficult, scary, impossible, disastrous situations) is the grips of your clubs being too fat, making it difficult to get a good hold on the club.

A close third is one in which you can't find your clubs and are being called to the tee at the US Open, the Masters, or your club championship final match.

Most Evasive Pseudo-Complimentary Assessment of a Poorly Designed Golf Course, "**It is the finest course of its kind I have ever played.**" The clever modifier is said to have been originated by Ben Hogan. But Gary Player, the quintessential public relations man, made it popular.

Most Bizarre Golf Invention, **A Putter with a Motor-Driven Propeller** on the top of the putter head that is activated by a switch on the grip. The idea is the whirring propeller will create a perfectly balanced stroke. It is not legal, but then, no one has ever produced one for mass, or even more than one, distribution. The only one of its kind is on display in the USGA Museum.

Most Clubs Broken in One Temper Tantrum, **Fourteen,** by the legendary Wilburn Artist "Lefty" Stackhouse, of Sequin, Texas, who confessed it himself to me. A small, wiry man and as quiet and gentle as a lamb when not at golf, Stackhouse had a storied on-course or otherwise golf-related temper. Of his many outbursts, breaking a full set of clubs over his knee, systematically starting with the driver and working down to the putter, was one of the least physically harmful to himself. He once hooked a drive into the woods, and when he found his ball up against a tree he went into a rage and began punching the tree with his right hand, the one he believed, correctly, was too active in his swing and caused the hooked shot. With each punch he growled to his hand, "Never again, ya sonovabitch." The hand swelled in response.

For all that, "Lefty" ran junior golf programs in his hometown that gave many young kids from the Latino neighborhoods an introduction to golf. He also inspired and helped start the careers of one fine professional who had some success on the Tour—Shelly Mayfield.

Largest Family of Golf Professionals, **Six**, the Turnesas. There were the brothers Joe, Mike, Jim, Frank, Phil, and Doug. Joe, the oldest, was runner-up to Bobby Jones in the 1926 US Open and lost to Walter Hagen in the final match of the 1927 PGA Championship. He played on three Ryder Cup teams and won a number of tournaments on the PGA Tour. Jim was runner-up to Sam Snead in the 1942 PGA Championship and won that title in 1952. The other four were club professionals. Then there was Willie, the seventh son of Mike Sr., who as the greenskeeper at the Knollwood CC, in White Plains, New York, introduced his seven sons to the game. Willie was the only one to remain an amateur. He was one of the best, winner of two US Amateur championships (1938, 1948), a British Amateur championship (1947), and played on three US Walker Cup teams.

Longest "Sandy" in a Major, **164 yards**, by the aptly named Sandy Lyle, who hit a 7-iron from a fairway bunker on the left side of the 18th hole at Augusta National GC to within ten feet and holed the putt for a birdie three to win the 1988 Masters by one shot.

▶ LEASTS

First Miniature Golf Course, **The Ladies Putting Club, St. Andrews, Scotland**, 1867. It was not what we associate with modern-day miniature golf—all the windmills, etc.—but it was effectively that. It was an eighteen-hole putting green called The Himalayas that exists to this day at the Old Course. Members of the R&A put it together for women who had become interested in golf but could not play the real game because the social norms of the time deemed it unacceptable for women to perform the "violent" movements of a golf swing.

The first miniature golf course as we know it was invented by James Barber, who introduced it in 1916 on his private estate near the Carolina Hotel, in Pinehurst, North Carolina. Barber called it Thistle Dhu (This Will Do). His wife designed the course obstacles, which had a fairyland theme. When in 1922 Thomas McCulloch Fairbairn developed an artificial green out of a mixture of cottonseed hulls, sand, oil, and dye (which were played on in a few early-day professional tournaments in the south), miniature golf courses sprouted up around the country and became something of a craze. At one time in the 1920s there were over 150 rooftop courses in New York City alone. These were fairly simple courses, but the idea of adding windmills and the like seems to have come in with the first commercial minigolf courses, which were introduced in 1927 and patented under the name Tom Thumbs by Garnet Carter. He put the first one atop Lookout Mountain, in Tennessee, as a diversion for guests at a hotel he operated.

Some of the most fantastic courses currently in play exist in Myrtle Beach, South Carolina.

Lowest Competitive Round Nontour or Championship, Fifty-five, by Homero Blancas in the 1962 Oil Premier Invitational, an amateur tournament in Longview, Texas. It was a nine-hole course that no longer exists (and the name of which is lost in the mists of history), each nine played from a different set of tees. It measured just over five thousand yards, enough to make it a more or less regulation course. Homero made thirteen birdies and one eagle on the par-70 layout, and used twenty putts. His nine-hole scores were 27–28. Blancas went on to play college golf for Houston University, then joined the PGA Tour in 1965 and was Rookie of the Year. He won four events on the PGA Tour and one on the Senior PGA (now Champions) Tour.

Youngest Canadian Open Champion, **Albert Murray**, 20 years, 10 months old, in 1908. He shot 300 at the Royal Montreal GC.

9 **college golf**

▷ **FIRSTS, MOSTS, AND LEASTS**

⚑ MEN: NCAA DIVISION ONE

First Division 1 Team Champions, **Yale**, 1897.

First Division 1 Individual Champion, **Louis Bayard Jr.** (Princeton, 1897).

Notable Others:

Chandler Egan	(Harvard, 1902)
Ellis Knowles	(Yale, 1907)
Robert Hunter	(Yale, 1910)
Jesse Sweetser	(Yale, 1920)
Watts Gunn	(Georgia Tech, 1920)
Tom Aycock	(Yale, 1929)
G. T. Dunlap	(Princeton, 1930–1931)
Walter Emery	(Oklahoma, 1933)
Charles Yates	(Georgia Tech, 1934)
Charles Kocsis	(Michigan, 1936)
Freddie Haas Jr.	(LSU, 1937)
Earl Stewart	(LSU, 1941)
Frank Tatum	(Stanford, 1942)
Wally Ulrich	(Carleton, 1943)
Bob Harris	(San Jose State, 1948)

Harvie Ward	(North Carolina, 1949)
Fred Wampler	(Purdue, 1950)
Tom Nieporte	(Ohio State, 1951)
Jim Vickers	(Oklahoma, 1952)
Hillman Robbins	(Memphis State, 1954)
Joe Campbell	(Purdue, 1955)
Rick Jones	(OSU, 1956)
Rex Baxter	(Houston, 1957)
Phil Rodgers	(Houston, 1958)
Dick Crawford	(Houston, 1959–1960)
Jack Nicklaus	(Ohio State, 1961)
Kermit Zarley	(Houston, 1962)
R. H. Sikes	(Arkansas, 1963)
Marty Fleckman	(Houston, 1965)
Bob Murphy	(Florida, 1966)
Hale Irwin	(Colorado, 1967)
Grier Jones	(Oklahoma State, 1968)
John Mahaffey	(Houston, 1970)
Ben Crenshaw	(Texas, 1971)
Ben Crenshaw and Tom Kite	(Texas, 1972)
Ben Crenshaw	(Texas, 1973)
Curtis Strange	(Wake Forest, 1974)
Jay Haas	(Wake Forest, 1975)
Scott Simpson	(USC, 1976–1977)
David Edwards	(OSU, 1978)
Gary Hallberg	(Wake Forest, 1979)
Jay Don Blake	(Utah State, 1980)
Billy Ray Brown	(Houston, 1982)
John Inman	(North Carolina, 1984)
Scott Verplank	(Oklahoma, 1986)
Phil Mickelson	(Arizona State, 1989, 1990, 1992)
Justin Leonard	(Texas, 1994)
Tiger Woods	(Stanford, 1996)
Luke Donald	(Northwestern, 1999)
Charles Howell III	(Oklahoma State, 2000)
Alejandro Canizares	(Arizona State, 2003)

First Non-Ivy League Division 1 Team Champions, Michigan, 1934.

First Non-Ivy League Division 1 Individual Champion, Fred Lamprecht (Tulane, 1924).

First Western States Division 1 Team Champions, Stanford, 1938.

First Western States Division 1 Individual Champion, Walter Emery (Oklahoma, 1933).

First Back-to-Back Division 1 Individual Champion, Dexter Cummings (Yale, 1923–1924).

Most Consecutive NCAA College Player-of-the-Year Awards Won, Three, by Ben Crenshaw, 1971–1973. He played for University of Texas.

First NAIA Team Champions, North Texas State, 1952.

First NAIA Individual Champion, Marion Hiskey, North Texas State, 1952.

First College Golf Scholarship, 1933, to Freddie Haas Jr. Haas was planning to take his college education in his home state, at the University of Arkansas. But when in Louisiana to play a regional tournament, he met Louisiana's colorful, historic governor, Huey Long. Long wanted to raise the identity of his state in every way possible and thought college golf was one good way to do so. He sweet-talked Haas, who had attained notice with his fine play in regional amateur tournaments, into coming to Louisiana State. He further sweetened the pot by offering Haas tuition. Haas couldn't resist, and he pioneered what, in effect, ended all semblance of Old World amateurism.

Haas would go on to win the 1937 NCAA Individual championship, and, when still an amateur, won the Memphis Open and halted Byron Nelson's famous streak of victories at eleven. Haas soon after turned pro and had a modest career on the Tour, winning four times and playing on one US Ryder Cup team. He also made contributions to the game through equipment innovations. (See **Equipment**.)

Of course, with the college golf scholarship the definition of amateur status was all but altered for all time, since receivers of the scholarship are being paid, in effect, to play golf. That aside, the college golf scholarship has been and continues to be one of the most influential innovations and American contributions to the development of high-quality competitive golf.

Finally, the college golf scholarship is unique to the United States, and it accounts in some part to the rise in the number of outstanding international golf champions. Many have tempered their games playing high-level American collegiate golf on scholarships. Luke Donald and Paul Casey are but two most recent examples.

 WOMEN—AIA

First Individual Winner, **Eleanor Dudley** (Alabama, 1941).

First AIA Team Champion, **Rollins College**, 1974.

 WOMEN—NCAA

First Team Champion, **Tulsa University**, 1982.

First Individual Champion, **Kathy Baker** (Tulsa University, 1982).

10 women's golf

▶ FIRSTS, MOSTS, AND LEASTS

First Woman Golfer, **Mary Queen of Scots.** Born Mary Stewart, she had an adventurous life, much of it dealing with intrigue revolving around the English royal throne. She was held exile in Scotland in the mid-1500s, and to pass some of her time she took up golf. There is no record of her competence at the game, but she was into it; she was on the course when notified that her husband, Lord Darnley, who she despised, had been murdered. It may not have come as a surprise to Mary, for she took the news and continued her game.

She is credited with giving us the term *caddie.* She used the French term and pronunciation, *cadet,* pronounced with a silent *t* (she was married for a time to the king of France) for young servants who do the carrying for their masters.

First British Woman's Amateur Champion, **Lady Margaret Scott,** 1893.

First Organizaton of Women Golfers, **The Fish Wives of Musselburgh,** 1810.

First (and to Date Only) Women's Private Golf Club, **Women's National Golf and Tennis Club.** Marion Hollins, a fine amateur golfer (winner of the 1922 US Women's Amateur championship), and a feminist well before the term came into the lexicon, organized the club in 1922 in Glen Head, New York (on Long Island). It had a fine clubhouse designed by the prestigious architectural firm of McKim, Mead, and White. Devereux Emmet, a prominent course designer at the time, built the course (with Hollins near at hand; she worked with Alister MacKenzie on the design of a couple of holes at Augusta National and was responsible for the fabulous par-3 16th at Cypress Point. She also was the driving force behind the creation of the highly regarded Pasatiempo GC, in Santa Cruz, California.). The course was meant to accommodate women in terms of the length they could, on average, hit the ball. But the central concept of the club was to relieve women who wanted to play golf from male dominance and proscription. It had as many as three hundred members, but in 1941, in the aftermath of the Great Depression and the coming of World War II, the club was merged into The Creek, a nearby men-only golf club to which many husbands of National women belonged. It went out of existence a few years later.

Hollins introduced the noted English golf teacher, Ernest Jones, to the United States when she hired him as the club's professional. Jones remained in the United States after the club closed down and became a storied teacher with his central theme, "Swing the Clubhead."

First US Woman's Amateur Champion (at Stroke Play), **Mrs. Charles S. Brown,** 1895. It was an eighteen-hole tournament. Mrs. Brown shot 132 and won by two strokes.

First Winner of the British and US Women's Amateur in Same Year, **Dorothy Campbell,** 1909.

First US Woman's Amateur Champion (at Match Play), Ms. Beatrix Hoyt, 1896.

First US Women's Open Champion, Patty Berg, 1946. The USGA did not conduct this championship, or the next six, but all are nonetheless considered National Women's Opens. The inaugural was conducted by the Women's PGA (which would become the LPGA) and the Spokane (Washington) Athletic Round Table. Berg won the qualifying medal, then defeated Betty Jameson in the finals, five and four. She took home $5,600.

First US Women's Open Champion (at Stroke Play), Betty Jameson, 1947. The format went to stroke play in this second renewal of the championship, and it has been played that way ever since. Jameson shot 295 to win by six strokes over two amateurs, Polly Riley and Sally Sessions. With this victory Jameson also became the *First Woman to Break 300 in Tournament Play*.

First to Win the Women's British and US Amateur Championships in the Same Year, Dorothy Campbell, a Briton, in 1909.

First to Win the Ladies' British Amateur, Lady Margaret Scott, in 1893.

First Woman to Win the British and US Women's/Ladies' Amateur in the Same Year, Dorothy Campbell, of Great Britain, in 1909.

Youngest Winner of the US Women's Amateur Championship, Kimberly Kim, who was 14 when she won the 2006 title.

Youngest Winner of an "Adult" USGA Championship, Michelle Wie, who was 13 when she won the 2003 US Women's Publinks title.

Youngest Qualifier for the US Women's Open, Alexis Thompson, who was 12 when she qualified for the 2007 championship. In the championship proper she shot 76–82 and missed the cut.

First to Break Par over Seventy-two Holes in US Women's Open, **Amy Alcott,** who had 280 (–4) when winning the 1980 championship, at Richland CC, Nashville, Tennessee. She won by nine strokes.

Oldest Winner of the US Women's Open, **Fay Crocker,** who was 40 when she won the 1955 championship.

Lowest Round in US Women's Open, 63 (–8), by Helen Alfredsson, in the 1994 US Women's Open, at the Saucon Valley CC in Pennsylvania.

Largest Margin of Victory in Final of US Women's Amateur Championship, **Thirteen and Twelve,** Glenna Collett over Miriam Burns Horn Jr. in 1928.

Longest Playoff for US Women's Open, **Twenty holes.** Se Ri Pak and Jenny Chuasiriporn were tied after the regulation eighteen-hole playoff, and Pak won it on the second sudden-death hole, 1998.

First Curtis Cup Match, **1932.** This is the women's version of the Walker Cup Matches, pitting the best amateurs from the United States and Great Britain. In the inaugural, the United States won, at Wentworth GC, England.

First USGA Girl's Junior Amateur Champion, **Marlene Bauer,** 1949. Bauer went on to help pioneer the Ladies Professional Golfers Association (LPGA).

Tallest Winner of the US Women's Open, **Carol Mann,** at 6'3."

First Woman to Compete against Men on PGA Tour, **Mildred "Babe" Didrikson, Zaharias.** The greatest and most versatile woman athlete of the twentieth century, Zaharias was a track and field standout in the 1932 Olympics, winning two gold medals and one silver, and was an outstanding baseball and basketball player. She took up golf in her twenties and soon became one of the top players on the women's pro circuit. Her first appearance against men pros was in the 1938 Los Angeles Open. She played as amateur and shot 81–84 and missed the cut.

However, in 1945 she played in three PGA Tour events. The first was the LA Open, where she made the thirty-six-hole cut but failed to make the third-round cut. In the Phoenix Open she completed the seventy-two-hole event with rounds of 77–72–75–80, which got her 33rd place. In Tucson Open the following week she again completed the seventy-two holes and had 307, which got her a tie for 44th. At Phoenix and Tucson she did not get a sponsor's exemption; she qualified on her own for the tournament proper in each, both times over thirty-six holes.

***First Woman Professional Photographed in the Nude (Presumably)*, Jan Stephenson,** 1986. Stephenson, an attractive Australian, posed in a bathtub filled with golf balls that covered all of her sexiest parts. The photograph was part of a campaign to sell Dunlop equipment, but also an effort to put some sex into the women's game.

Stephenson had a flair for self-promotion, as her posing for this ad would indicate, but she was also a fine golfer. She won sixteen times on the LPGA Tour, including three majors: the US Women's Open (1983), the LPGA Championship (1982), and the DuMaurier Classic (1981).

***Youngest to Win Three LPGA Majors*, Yani Iseng,** born in 1989, won the 2008 LPGA Championship, the 2009 Kraft Nabisco Championship, and the 2010 British Women's Open.

***Oldest Winner of an LPGA Tournament*, Beth Daniel,** who was 46 years, 8 months, 29 days, when she won the 2003 Canadian Women's Open.

Oldest First-Time Winner on LPGA Tour, Fay Crocker, who was 40 years, 6 months, 18 days, when she won the 1955 Serbin Open.

Lowest Seventy-two-Hole Winning Score on LPGA Tour (in Relation to Par), 261 (–27), Annika Sorenstam, 2001 Standard Register PING. Moon Valley CC, Phoenix, par-72.

Lowest Seventy-two-Hole Winning Score on LPGA Tour (Raw Score), 258 (–22), Karen Stupples, in 2004 Welsch's/Fry's Championship. Dell Ulrich GC, Tucson, par-70.

Most Birdies in One Round of an LPGA Event, Thirteen, by Annika Sorenstam, 2001 Standard Register PING tournament. Her score for the round, 59 (see below).

Lowest Single-Round Score on LPGA Tour, 59 (–13), by Annika Sorenstam, in 2001 Standard Register PING, at Moon Valley CC, Phoenix, Arizona, par-72.

Most Career Professional Tournament Victories, Eighty-eight, by Kathy Whitworth.

Most LPGA Tournaments Won in Single Year, Thirteen, by Mickey Wright, in 1963.

Most LPGA Majors Won in One Season, Three, Babe Zaharias. 1950 US Women's Open, Titleholders, and Western Open. *Only three majors were held in 1950.*

Most LPGA Championships Won, Four, Mickey Wright.

Most Career Majors Won, Fifteen, Patty Berg.

Most Straightforward Description of the Effects of the Menstrual Cycle on Women Golfers. Joanne Carner, one of the best woman golfers of all time, was always known for candor, and when asked about the effects of the menstrual cycle on her golf she did not hesitate to respond with a telling anecdote. "Oh, that was the worst.

My hands would get huge, because you retain water, and you don't have any feel. It often came for me around US Open time. At Tulsa in 1983 I opened with 81, on my period, feet and hands swollen, five pounds heavier, whole body logy. Then it was over, and I followed up with 70, 72, and 68 [low round in the tournament] and lost by a stroke to Jan Stephenson." Carner never hinted that Jan Stephenson won that year by default, but as a winner of five major titles, including two US Women's Opens and forty-three victories on the LPGA Tour, and of course a golfer not likely to shoot in the 80s, one can make a case that if not for her period she might well have had that 1983 Open by at least a stroke.

Most US Women's Open Victories, **Four**, Betsy Rawls, Mickey Wright.

Most Consecutive LPGA Wins, **Four**, Mickey Wright, in 1962; Heart of America Invitational, Albuquerque Swing Parade, Salt Lake City Open, and Spokane Open.

Wright was the first to set this record. Subsequently, Wright did it again, in 1963, and it has also been done by Kathy Whitworth (1969), Annika Sorenstam (2001), and Lorena Ochoa (2008).

Oldest Player to Make Cut on LPGA Tour, **Joanne Carner**, 64 years, 26 days, in 2002 LPGA Takefuji Classic.

Most Consecutive Cuts Made on LPGA Tour, **229**, by Jane Blalock, between 1969 and 1980. She won twenty-nine of the tournaments, but none of them a major.

Most Consecutive Years with a Victory, **Seventeen**, Kathy Whitworth (1962–1978).

Most LPGA Players in a Sudden-Death Playoff, **Six**. At Jamie Farr Kroger Classic, Se Ri Pak defeated Carin Koch, Kelli Kuehne, Mardi Lunn, Sherri Steinhauer, and Karrie Webb on the first extra hole, with a birdie.

Longest LPGA Sudden-Death Playoff, **Ten holes.** Joe Ann Prentice defeated Sandra Palmer and Kathy Whitworth in 1972 Corpus Christi Civitan Open.

Biggest Comeback to Victory on LPGA Tour, **Ten strokes,** by Mickey Wright in 1964 Tall City Open. Annika Sorenstam did it in 2001 in The Office Depot, and so did Louise Friberg in the 2008 MasterCard Classic.

First Amateur to Defeat the Pros, **Polly Riley,** the 1950 Tampa Open. Others who did this: Pat O'Sullivan, 1951 Titleholders Championship; Catherine LaCoste, 1967 US Women's Open; and JoAnne Carner, 1969 Burdine Invitational.

First Solheim Cup Competition, **1990.** The women's equivalent of the Ryder Cup Matches, the cup is named after Karsten Solheim, founder of PING, the golf equipment maker, who was a strong supporter of women's golf. It is a biennial competition between US and European women professionals.

First Solheim Cup Team Captains, **Kathy Whitworth (US), Mickey Walker (Eur).**

Oldest Solheim Cup Competitors, **Juli Inkster (US),** 49 years, 1 month, 28 days, in 2009; **Laura Davies (Eur),** 45 years, 10 months, 16 days, in 2009.

Youngest Solheim Cup Competitors, **Paula Creamer (US),** 19 years, 1 month, 4 days, in 2005; **Suzann Petteresen (Eur),** 21 years, 5 months, 13 days, in 2002.

Youngest Winner on LPGA Tour, **Marlene Bauer Hagge,** the 1952 Sarasota Open, an eighteen-hole event, at 18 years, 14 days.

Youngest Winner of a Major, **Morgan Pressel,** 18 years, 10 months, 9 days, when she won the 2007 Kraft Nabisco Championship.

Record Lowest One-Year Scoring Average, **68.696**, Vare Trophy, Annika Sorenstam, 2004.

Most Vare Trophy Wins, **Seven**, Kathy Whitworth (1965–1967, 1969, 1972).

Most Consecutive Rounds in the 60s, **Fourteen**, Annika Sorenstam.

Most Rounds in 60s in One Season, **Fifty-one**, Lorena Ochoa, 2004.

Most Prize Money Earned in One Year, **$4,364,994**, Lorena Ochoa, 2007.

Most Money Earned, Career, **$22,573,192**, Annika Sorenstam.

First Woman on USGA Executive Committee, **Judy Bell**.

First International to Win the US Women's Open, **Catherine LaCoste**, 1967.

11 **equipment**

▷ FIRSTS, MOSTS, AND LEASTS

First Dimpled Golf Ball, **1905**. It was the first concave dimple and the prototype of that used on today's balls. It was invented and patented by an Englishman, William Taylor, in 1908. The covers of golf balls up to this time had small, raised protrusions called brambles. After some use these pimplelike protrusions would be mashed flat, which reduced the ability to control their flight. However, that wasn't Taylor's main concern, as his son wrote in *Golf Illustrated* magazine in 1987. Taylor wanted to prolong the useful life of golf balls. By turning the brambles inside out and turning them into dimples the golf club would strike the larger rather than the smaller radius of the ball. No mashed pimples, which brings up a nice irony. In experimenting with his idea Taylor used a blackhead remover to scoop out the brambles and create a dimple. It was an almost instant success, and soon after all golf balls would be made with concave dimples.

First Wooden Tee, **1899**, invented by Dr. George Grant, an African American dentist from Boston, Massachusetts, whose parents were escaped southern slaves. He received a patent for his tee but never promoted the device and let the patent lapse. His motivation was the way balls were teed up at the time. That is, golfers took pinches of moist sand and built a mound from it on which their ball was propped. A box full of such sand was in place at every tee, which may be why to this day the teeing ground is often referred to as the tee-box. In any case, the mounding played hell on one's hands, which did not inspire a patient's confidence in his dentist.

Grant's tee was a stubby device, the top third slightly less wide than the longer base. It had a round, rubber cup at the top. It gained little to no attention at the time, mainly because Grant didn't try to sell it. Ten years later, however, another dentist, Dr. William Lowell, of Maplewood, New Jersey, picked up on Grant's idea and created his version of a wooden tee, which in design is closer to the one we use today—except it was much shorter.

Lowell's tee was made of white birch wood, and the cup was painted red; hence, the Reddy Tee, the name Lowell gave it. An entrepreneur, Lowell sought to make his fortune with his Reddy Tee and marketed it vigorously. His coup was to get the popular champion, Walter Hagen, to use it. As a result the Reddy Tee gained enormous exposure and relegated the sand-filled tee-boxes to a thing of the past. However, many imitations arose. In 1931 alone close to one hundred patents were issued on golf tees. Lowell spent years and considerable legal fees fighting what he deemed were infringements on his patent, and he never did cash in on his Reddy Tee. However, he did leave the game with a handy device.

The term *tee*, some believe, derives from an Old Scottish word *teaz*, which has a Latin root that means "support or prop." Could be. My research indicates the term derives from the Greek for the letter *T*, *tau*, which was once used as we now use *X*, to mark the spot or place where things begin.

***First Golf Professional to Sign an Equipment Endorsement Contract*, Harry Vardon.** Vardon's historic, groundbreaking tour of the United States in 1900 has been credited with generating great interest in golf in America, where the game was still in its infancy. It did that, but there was also a financial interest very much to the point. Spalding, the American sporting goods manufacturer, had come out with a new ball, called the Vardon Flyer. The tour by the acknowledged best golfer in the world was meant to generate sales in the United States. Vardon not only played exhibition matches on golf courses, he put on clinics in department stores, where he hit Vardon Flyers into netting. Vardon was bored stiff in the department stores, but he enjoyed the exhibition matches. And, while in the country he won the US Open.

Just how successful Vardon's tour was in terms of Vardon Flyers sold is unknown. Being it was a guttie, sales must surely have been stunted by the introduction in that same year of the much livelier Haskell ball. Indeed, the Haskell took over the game almost immediately. In any case, there is no record of a golf professional before Vardon contracted to play a particular brand of golf equipment.

***The First Steel Shaft*, 1893**. It was made by Thomas Horsburgh, a Scottish blacksmith. He received a patent on it, which he allowed to lapse because he couldn't get anyone interested in it. It was solid steel, and, while reasonably flexible, weighed a ton, figuratively speaking.

A. F. Knight, an engineer with General Electric in Schenectady, New York, patented a more viable steel shaft in 1910. Knight's shaft was a tube of steel, which was getting close to the final solution. But it didn't catch on commercially. The same fate fell on the perforated tubular steel shaft patented in 1915 by Allan Lard, of Washington, D.C. The perforations were meant to reduce torque, or twisting, during the swing.

One reason these last two shafts failed to gain any purchase was because golf's two ruling bodies, the USGA and the R&A,

were beginning to get involved in the approval of equipment and resisted them. No specific reason was given, and golfers continued to play with hickory-shafted clubs. Nevertheless, the idea of a steel shaft persisted, and in the early 1920s a British fishing rod manufacturer, Apollo, produced the first really playable one. However, the tube was closed with a welded overlap that made for inconsistent performance; it was also deemed unattractive. It didn't catch on. These problems were overcome at around the same time by the Bristol Steel Company in Connecticut. Bristol engineers devised a way to make a seamless tubular shaft, which made a big difference. It became the gold standard.

Now it was a matter of getting the golf authorities to approve it, which wasn't easy. The Bristol people were determined, and clever. They hired a golf professional named Harry Lagerblade, who knew that the Western Golf Association, the second-oldest such association in American golf, was a bitter rival of the USGA. The WGA saw the USGA as "eastern elitist" and believed it instead should be the dominant association in America. Hence, the WGA was always looking for ways to upset the USGA's apple cart. To that end, in April 1922 in Chicago, Lagerblade demonstrated the Bristol shaft to the president of the WGA, Albert Gates. Amateur champion Chick Evans, and professional star, Jock Hutchison, hit the shots. Evans and Hutchison felt there was no difference between steel and hickory in respect to accuracy, distance, or steel's "ability to overcome a bad swing." However, that first test was made on a cold, windy day. A month later, on a nicer day, the test was made again, and while there was no report from the demonstrators this time, Gates approved their use in all WGA tournaments, beginning in 1922.

However, while the USGA allowed the use of steel in a few of its lesser tournaments in order to assess them, it did not give total approval until 1926. The R&A was slower, finally approving in

1930. Thus, when the 1929 Ryder Cup Match was played in England the Americans were required to use hickory-shafted clubs. Most had been playing steel for the past few years, and the switching back may well have led to the US team losing the match.

First Steel Shaft Used in US Open, 1924. It was allowed in putters. The winner, Cyril Walker, used one.

First Winner of the US Open Using a Full Set of Steel-Shafted Clubs, Billy Burke, 1931. It may have been a good thing Burke, and the runner-up, George Von Elm, were playing steel shafts. Hickory might not have lasted through it all. They were tied after the regulation seventy-two holes, and in the thirty-six-hole playoff tied again. In yet another thirty-six-hole playoff Burke finally prevailed, at the Inverness GC, Toledo, Ohio. (See under **USGA Championships Mosts.**)

The First Seamless Step-down Tapered Steel Shaft, 1929. The True Temper Company developed a technique by which they could reduce the outer diameter of shafts by creating a step-down pattern that tapered them as they ran into the clubhead. The idea was to help golfers get more loft on their shots, always an issue with average golfers. What's more, they could vary the space between steps so the loft could be adjusted to every golfer's particular requirements.

First Graphite Shaft, 1969. Since the advent of the steel shaft, there had been efforts to make golf shafts lighter so clubs could be swung with greater speed, thus producing more distance. To that end, the Shakespeare Sporting Goods Company had been making fiberglass golf shafts since 1947. But they did not gain a large following. However, in the mid-1960s Royal Aircraft Ltd. had been experimenting with carbon fiber, which led to the development of the graphite golf shaft. It is composed of threads of graphite bound together. In 1969 Shakespeare introduced its version, which was developed by a staff engineer named Frank Thomas. At the same time, James Flood, an aircraft engineer in California, who had also been experimenting with graphite, produced and marketed his Aldila graphite golf shaft and formed a company under that name that exists to this day.

Frank Thomas, who would become the USGA's Technical Director in charge of approving (or disallowing) all equipment innovations, has been credited in some circles with the invention, but Flood does not buy it.

The First Golf Bag, **1890.** Until then golfers themselves, or a hired caddie, carried the entire set of their clubs in a bunch under their arms. However, Dr. B. J. Traill, a resident of St. Andrews, Scotland, had grown tired of his caddies often dropping the clubs, either because they were aging or had been drinking too much (or both). Traill asked his wife to sew up a canvas sack suitable for holding clubs. A strap was attached, and *voila!*

The First Cup in a Hole (date uncertain, probably the **mid-1800s**). Golf holes had long been pits in the ground often formed by golfers digging their heels into the turf. These holes broke down regularly, and the constant rebuilding became tiresome. Something had to be done, and it came to pass, according to Laurie Aucherterlonie, that "drain tiles and some chimney stacks of the time were clay or ceramic and odds and ends of them were deemed the perfect liner [for a golf hole]. They happened to be 4¼ inches [in diameter]. Too bad they weren't six inches," Auchterlonie, a poor putter, opined. In any case, that became the accepted size of a golf hole, and has been the regulation ever since. When cast-iron pipes were manufactured at that size, the Crail Golf Club, up the coast from St. Andrews, was the first to slip them into its holes.

The First Numbered Irons, **1926 (approximately).** "Wild" Bill Mehlhorn, a pioneer American golf professional, claimed to have put numbers on irons for the first time. In the book, *Gettin' to the Dance Floor, an Oral History of American Golf,* Mehlhorn told of redesigning iron heads, and to cap his work he also changed their designation from names to number. "The heads on irons were too thin and long, so I cut a quarter-inch off the end and soldered it on the back to make it heavy enough. I took it to Forgan, the clubmaker in Scotland, because one of the cleek makers there had caddied for me [in the prototype Ryder Cup Match]. I asked him if he could make a set of clubs like it. He said sure. It took him a week to hammer them out. Instead of names I put numbers on them, because it was easier."

First American Golf Equipment Manufacturer, **A. J. Spalding,** which brought out its first set of clubs in 1894.

First Use of the Copying Lathe to Produce Wood Heads, **1897.** For centuries, wooden-headed golf clubs were manufactured entirely by hand, craftsmen shaping thick blocks of wood using saws and files, chisels and hammers. That slow, laborious process went the way of the dinosaurs around 1897 when a Yankee carpenter noticed Scottish-born golf professional Robert White fashioning a wood in the traditional way in his shop at the Myopia Hunt Club, in Massachusetts. In an article in a 1956 issue of *Golfdom* magazine, White, an American golf pioneer, recalled the incident.

> Watching White sweat over his work, the carpenter said to him, "I always thought the Scots were smart, but they must be damn fools. There's a shoe factory over at Lynn [Mass.] that could do that wood job of yours in two or three minutes."

White gave the carpenter, Tom Gardner, a chance to match deed to word, and said later, "The fellow turned out some beautiful heads." Gardner did the work on a copying lathe, which was used in shoe manufacture to produce lasts. Lynn was a major shoemaking center in the United States at the time. The copying lathe was taken up by all golf club manufacturers, which quickly led to the mass production of more reasonably priced woods. As with the development of the rubber-core, three-piece golf ball, the copying lathe significantly expanded participation in golf and stimulated its growth.

First Surlyn-Covered, Two-Piece Golf Ball, **1967.** Surlyn, developed by DuPont, is an extremely abrasion-resistant and durable synthetic material, characteristics especially desirable for the majority of golfers, who often strike the ball in its middle or upper part. With the balata ball these mishits put cuts or gashes in the cover and render them useless. Surlyn doesn't cut. The Ram Company, a golf equipment manufacturer, was the first to see the future and produced the first Surlyn-covered ball. It was called the 3-D, for distance, durability, and dependability. It was not a success, mainly because the cover was too thick.

In 1970, the Spalding golf division brought out a Surlyn-covered ball called the Top-Flite, which did work. It had a solid core beneath its cover. It didn't cut, of course, but Spalding's main peddle point was that it went farther.

First Metal "Wood" Used on the PGA Tour, **1979.** Drivers and perhaps a spoon or two made of metal—either aluminum-magnesium or steel—had been in golf since the late 1800s. They were made by the Standard Mills Company, in Sunderland, Scotland, which sold some one million of their solid aluminum heads from 1895 through 1939.

In the United States aluminum heads, because of their durability and lower cost, were found almost exclusively at commercial driving ranges. They were made available by range owners for beginner golfers who didn't yet own a set of clubs, or for those simply out to have some fun whacking balls. Either way, the clubs took a terrific beating but held up for a long time. Wooden woods would not have made it past a weekend.

As noted above, it was the advent of the Surlyn-covered golf ball that brought the metal "wood" into common use. At that time, Gary Adams was working for the Wittek Company, a major supplier of driving range equipment. At a long-drive contest he was monitoring, three different ball brands were used. Two were made of conventional balata, one was the new Spalding (Surlyn-covered) Top-Flite. All the contestants were using persimmon drivers—a wood wood. Adams discovered on the ground that Spalding's pitch that Top-Flite was the longest ball in the game wasn't the case. Indeed, it came up shorter than the balata balls. Adams's curiosity was tweaked. He read the small print in the Spalding advertisements for its Top-Flite and found the answer to the puzzle. It said the Top-Flite was longer *off the second shot*, which was to say, when hit with an iron. Eureka! Adams put two and two together. He perceived that the Surlyn-covered ball when hit *with steel* was the combination that produced the greater distance. He made some tests on his own (he was a low-handicap golfer) hitting balata and Surlyn balls with a 5-iron. Sure enough, Surlyn now went farther.

Adams went into business, forming the TaylorMade Golf Company. He understood that equipment tour pros played helped immensely to make it popular among the general golfing public, and he set about designing a metal driver that the pros would use. This involved, in large part, the club looking good. With Eddie Langert, his main club designer, he produced a driver with a head shape and face line very close to the legendary Mac-Gregor woods. The pros showed some interest but were especially attracted to another characteristic intrinsic to what Adams called the Tour Burner. It was hollow within (solid metal would be far too heavy), so weight distribution could be manipulated. The ideal location for putting the most weight was at the bottom of the head. With this lower center of gravity a good player could hit a driver off the ground (not teed up). Indeed, that's when it really took off. The first metal driver, with twelve degrees of loft, was first put into PGA Tour play in the 1979 MONY Tournament of Champions, by Ron Streck and Jim Simons. But they used it as a 3-wood, or metal, or spoon. Bingo! The pros could use the Tour Burner driver off the fairway, which made the greens of par-5s more accessible in two shots.

For all that, the tour pros didn't immediately flock to the metal driver. Some were tradition bound, others were tied up by contracts with other equipment manufacturers. However, when **Ron Streck** became the *First to Win a Pro Tour Event with a Metal Driver*—the 1981 Michelob-Houston Open—interest was greatly stirred.

But when Lee Trevino, one of the best golfers in the game, won the 1984 PGA championship using the TaylorMade driver, the wood wood began a pretty swift departure into the dustbin of golf history.

The First Rubber-Core, Three-Piece Golf Ball, 1898.

In that year Coburn Haskell, an avid but poor golfer, was browsing about the Goodrich Rubber Company plant in Akron, Ohio, while waiting for his friend, Bertram Work, an employee at the company, to join him in a round of golf. Haskell spotted some bands of waste rubber on the floor and thought they could be wound into a golf ball as lively as tennis balls, which were made of the same material. With Work's considerable assistance, Haskell had rubber thread wound very tightly around a solid core and covered it all with, at first, gutta percha, the rubberlike material of the ball then in use. Thus, three piece. When Haskell began using balata for the cover at the suggestion of Work, the real difference was made.

After a Goodrich shop foreman named John Gammeter invented a machine to wind the cores, the Haskell ball went into production and became an almost instant success. It was indeed very lively compared to the solid-state guttie, which pleased golfers of all stripes, and it was also much cheaper to produce. It was called the Haskell, but it was often referred to as the "Bounding Billy" for how far it traveled once it hit the ground. Not only that, it was much easier on the hands at contact with the ball—no more shock with a mishit. And those poorly hit balls would go much farther than the relatively lifeless guttie. In all, the Haskell ball was perhaps the most revolutionary invention in golf's long history. It made golf more fun, even if it didn't lower someone's score, and in the end brought an exponential growth in the game.

First Major Victory with the Haskell Ball, 1902, when Alexander "Sandy" Herd used it to win the British Open. Harry Vardon and others continued to use the guttie (Vardon until 1914), but the younger generation took the Haskell up quickly after Herd's victory.

First Rubber Grip, 1937. Golf grips had for centuries been made of various forms of leather. In damp weather and when the hands sweated in hot weather they would become slippery. No one thought to do anything serious about this issue until Jack Burke Sr. got an idea when his car had a flat tire. Burke was a pioneer American golf professional from Philadelphia who came close to winning an early US Open, but he made his career, mostly in Houston, as a highly respected golf teacher. His son, Jack Jr., would become one of the finest golfers in the game, winner of a Masters and PGA championship and numerous tour events. Jack Jr. told how his father invented the rubber grip in the book *Gettin' to the Dance Floor, an Oral History of American Golf.*

> Dad signed a lot of clubs for MacGregor in the early days, and invented the all-weather grip, that rubber grip with a heavy cord of cotton running through it. That was when the grips went from leather to rubber. In fact, he had the patent on it. Henry Picard, Craig Wood, Ben Hogan and Jimmy Demaret were the partners he put into the company we had here in Houston; Burke Par, it was called. He got the idea for it when a tire on his car blew out one day. He saw how the cord was wrapped up in those tires. He used to lose the club at the top of his backswing and always blamed the leather grips, so he wanted something better to hold on to, and saw the answer in that blown-out rubber tire. He made a grip he could use in any kind of weather, and could keep it tacky by just scrubbing it down with soap and water when it got slippery from dirt and use. Picard was the first to use it on the Tour, then Hogan did and it became very popular. When dad died the company sort of went down and the patents ran out and everybody started making the rubber-cord grip. Then just all-rubber ones.

The Golf Pride Company was formed in the early 1950s to produce rubber grips and became the world leader in their manufacture.

First Legal Sand Wedge, **1931–1932.** In the late 1920s a Texan named Edwin Kerr McClain designed a club for playing shots out of greenside bunkers. It had a 9-iron loft, but more importantly the entire back of the club head was a rounded mass of metal. Its weight was such that the club could drive down into the sand behind the ball and create enough force to propel the ball up and forward. Up to that time golfers used a thin-bladed niblick

(9-iron) for the shot and usually tried to pick the ball out cleanly. The ball had to be sitting up nicely to pull that off, and it usually didn't. Or, they could try hitting behind the ball slightly and force it out that way. One way or the other, it was a very difficult to keep that knifelike blade from digging too deeply into the sand. When it did, the ball usually stayed in the bunker. In all, not even the best players in the game were very good at playing out of sand traps. The McClain sand wedge was the solution, and it got off to a fine start when Bobby Jones used it to play a crucial shot from a bunker on his way to winning the 1930 British Open, the third leg of his famous Grand Slam. However, McClain's sand wedge had a concave clubface and could conceivably and sometimes in fact did hit the ball twice with one stroke. For that reason, in 1931 it was deemed illegal. Enter Gene Sarazen and the legal sand wedge.

Although he never acknowledged being influenced by Mc-Clain's sand wedge, Sarazen surely had to have been. What he did was refine the basic concept. He made it lighter—McClain's weighed twenty-five ounces—but most importantly, his had a flat face. Sarazen had at least two versions of what inspired his innovation. One, when flying in a small plane he noticed that when the pilot pulled back on the control stick the rear of the plane dipped down as the nose rose. Two, when watching a goose land on water its rear end hit first with its head raised.

Both described the basic principle behind the more sophisticated sand wedge that Sarazen designed. In his workshop he built up a wide flange on the rear of a niblick that was similar to the McClain version, but angled it so the backmost part hit the sand before the leading edge. That angle is what came to be known as the "bounce." Now there was far less chance of the club digging too deeply into the sand. The ball, as with the McClain version, is propelled up and out not entirely by contact with the clubface itself. The force of the moving sand is very much part of the process.

Sarazen put his sand wedge into play for the first time in the 1932 British Open. He recalled once that during practice rounds he was getting down in two from the bunkers so regularly and with such seeming ease the gallery began to wonder what sort of weapon he was using. Shrewdly aware of how the conservative R&A rules makers might react to his club, Sarazen put it upside down in his golf bag during his practice rounds and took it home every night under his long topcoat. He was convinced that the R&A would have barred it if they had noticed it prior to the start of the tournament. Using the wedge to great advantage, Sarazen won that 1932 Open.

It has been estimated that Sarazen's wedge took two strokes off the handicap of every golfer in the game when it was introduced, and still does. Sarazen, by the way, never made a dime off his innovation. His contract with Wilson Sporting Goods said that anything he devised in the way of equipment belonged to the company.

First Golf Car(t), **1951.** Merle Williams, a California businessman, started the manufacture of electric golf carts. The idea for an electricity-driven vehicle derived from World War II, when gas rationing was in effect. Williams began producing his carts in Redlands, California. Although decried by golf traditionalists, the golf cart has become an integral part of the game, allowing older people to continue playing long after they might have had to quit.

Most Clubs Carried by a Tournament Golfer, **Twenty-six (sometimes even more)**, Lawson Little, among others. In 1938 the USGA placed a limit on the number of clubs a golfer could carry in its competitions—fourteen. The Masters went along with the ruling. However, the PGA Tour set the limit at sixteen until 1949, when it also complied with the fourteen-club limit.

First Thread-Winding Machine for Manufacture of Golf Balls, **1900.** As noted in the entry on the first three-piece rubber-core ball, the Haskell, John Gammeter, a shop foreman for the Goodrich Tire Company, invented the machine to replace the much slower, labor-intensive winding done by hand. Gammeter's machine allowed for mass production of the ball.

First Machine to Measure Clubhead Speed, **1932.** Engineers at General Electric, in Schenectady, New York, created it.

First Center-Shafted Mallet Putter, **1903.** All putters before this one were thin-bladed and had the shaft attached at the heel. A. F. Knight, of Schenectady, New York, a poor putter himself, hit on the idea of a larger mallet head with the shaft centered atop it. His notion was that this would be a more stable putter and would propel the ball with more force while maintaining a smooth stroke, an important issue on the very slow greens of the time. It worked for Knight, but it worked even better for Walter Travis Jr., the best amateur in American golf at the time. With his "Schenectady," as the putter would come to be called, Travis won his third US Amateur Championship in 1903, and then the 1904 British Amateur. Afterward, the putter became very popular.

Most Bizarre Golf Invention. There are many zanies to choose from. We select a putter that has a motor, a push button to activate it, and a flywheel on the toe of the clubhead. The flywheel spinning is meant to provide a gyroscopic effect that keeps the blade square during the stroke. It's on display in the USGA Museum. It never went to market.

Longest Driver Ever Put into Tournament Play, **Fifty-two inches.** It was (is) wielded by "Rocky" Thompson, now a Senior Tour player.

First Nonmetal Golf Spikes, **1992**. The plastic cleat was developed by Faris McMullen and Ernie Deacon, who patented it under the name SoftSpike. It had an immediate impact on the game. Mainly, it solved the issue of small but bothersome clots of turf that were brought to the surface of greens by the sharp-pointed metal spikes that had been the convention for at least a century. Course maintenance supervisors were especially pleased, as were the owners of courses and members of private clubs; they kept the putting surfaces much smoother. This also took the USGA off the hook in regard to its long-standing rule against tapping down those clots of turf when they were in a golfer's line of putt. While the plastic cleat has become required at most golf courses, some tour pros, including Tiger Woods, continue to use metal spikes, citing greater stability.

First Grooved Iron, **1908**. Iron-headed clubs had until then always been smooth faced. The Haskell ball that was introduced in 1898 very quickly became the standard because it gave much greater distance than the gutta-percha, or "guttie," that was then in use. However, it was also more difficult to control, especially with irons. This stirred inventors. The solution was to sink grooves into the irons, which produced backspin to the ball when struck. E. Burr, of England, is credited with patenting this innovation, which he called "rib-facing." The grooves were approximately ¼ inch wide and separated by about two inches. From that time on the width, depth, and space between grooves would be a controversial issue.

First Use of Power-Driven Machinery to Build a Golf Course, **1931**. Alister MacKenzie used trenchers, tractors, and power shovels in constructing the Bayside Links, on Long Island, New York.

First Bulge Built into Face of a Driver, **1890s to early 1900s**. Drivers began to be made with a slightly curved, or convex face. The faces were flat, until then. The first driver with a bulge was called "The Bulger," of course. The invention is credited to an amateur golfer in England by name of Henry Lamb. Whether he used science in his work is not known, but it has been proven scientifically that the bulge reduces hooking and slicing through a mechanical effect called "gearing." Hit the ball toward the toe or heel and the face will turn in or out respectively, thus correcting to some degree a ball that would otherwise slice or hook a lot more. Eventually, roll was added to bulge. Roll is a shaping of the clubface with a slight contour from top to bottom. Bulge is a contour from the toe to the heel. Hence, bulge and roll. It is especially helpful for high handicap players who don't regularly hit the ball on the sweet spot—in the very center of the face.

Ben Hogan, however, was so certain he would hit the ball on the sweet spot he filed down the bulge and roll on his drivers; he liked a flat face. When the first metal drivers came out they didn't have bulge and roll, but after a few years a way was found to provide it.

12 media, the arts, etc.

▶ FIRSTS, MOSTS, AND LEASTS

First Written History of Golf, *Golf, A Royal Ancient Game*, by R & R Clark, Edinburgh, 1875.

First Book of Golf Instruction, *The Golfer's Manual: Being a Historical & Descriptive Account of the National Game of Scotland*, with an Appendix, by A Keen Hand. Published in 1857 by Whitehead & Orr. Keen Hand was Henry Brougham Farnie. The first "considerable excursion into [golf swing] theory," according to Herbert Warren Wind, is ***The Art of Golf*,** by Sir Walter Simpson, published in 1887.

First Book on the Mental Side or Psychology of Golf, *The Mystery of Golf*, by Arnold Haultain, 1908.

First Golf Periodical, *Golf, A Weekly Record of "Ye Royal and Ancient Game*," appeared for the first time in 1890.

First American Golf Periodical, *Golf Magazine*, began publication in 1898 with a yearly subscription rate of $1.

First American Periodical Devoted to Business of Golf, *Golfdom*, 1927.

First Golf Writers Association, **1938**. The Association of Golf Writers was originated by thirty British golf writers while attending the Walker Cup Matches that year. The first president was Bernard Darwin, a nephew of the famed naturalist. The Golf Writers Association of America was the second such organization. It was founded in 1946.

First National Golf Exhibition and Merchandise Show, **1926**, in Chicago.

First Instruction Manual on How to Caddy, **"How to Caddy,"** by Ernest A. Baughman, 1914.

First Use of High-Speed Sequence Photography of the Golf Swing, **1919**, for "Picture Analysis of Golf Strokes," an instructional description by Jim Barnes.

First Instruction Book with Photography, The Art of Golf, by Sir Walter Simpson, 1887.

First Golf Book Published in the United States, Golf in America: A Practical Guide, 1895, by James Lee.

First Play-by-Play Radio Broadcast of Golf Competition, **1930 US Open**. The announcer was Ted Husing.

First Golf Television Program, Pars, Birdies and Eagles, 1949. It took the form of a half-hour program and was developed and produced by two Chicago public-fee golf course operators, Joe Jemsek and Charles Nash. It was shown only on a local Chicago station and consisted of instruction delivered by such local club professionals as Johnny Revolta and Jimmy Hines. In another segment Jemsek, a PGA professional, explained rules of golf based on questions sent in by area golfers. Jemsek also conducted interviews with notable tour players when they happened to be in the Chicago area.

Nationally Televised Pro Tour Event, The Tam O'Shanter "World" Championship, 1953. There had already been two or three local telecasts of golf tournaments, most notably the 1947 US Open, in St. Louis. In 1953, however, the ABC network, just starting up its television branch and looking for something special to get attention, thought the Tam O'Shanter tournament, with its then stunningly high $25,000 first prize—more than double the *total* purse of any other tournament—would do the trick. Harry Wismer, a famous sports broadcaster at the time who was working for ABC, told the Tam O'Shanter tournament's promoter, George S. May, that ABC would televise May's event for $32,000. May agreed (needless to say, it was the *First* and *Last Time a Tournament Sponsor Paid a Network to Cover An Event*), and ABC set up a single camera atop the grandstand behind the 18th green for one-hour coverage of the last round. As luck would have it, one of the most spectacular shots ever played was caught on camera. The last player on the course with a chance to tie or win the tournament, Lew Worsham, holed a 102-yard second shot on the final hole for an eagle two to defeat Chandler Harper by one shot. Approximately one million people in fifteen states around the country (according to A. C. Nielsen) saw "The Shot." An excited George May immediately announced that the next year he would offer a $50,000 first prize for the tournament. And more importantly, in terms of popularizing golf, the following year the US Open began to be telecast nationally, followed three years later by the Masters, then the PGA Championship. At the same time, independent producers began telecasting regular tour events, and as a result golf became one of the country's most popular sports attractions. Golf had entered the Age of Television.

First Made-for-Television Golf Competition, All-Star Golf, 1954. Once again, Joe Jemsek had a hand in pioneering golf via television. He and a friend, Pete DeMet, had been toying with the idea of creating a series of man-to-man golf matches for television. It had a kind of forerunner in DeMet's television production of *All-Star Bowling*, which had been successful. Lew Worsham's miracle wedge shot at Tam O'Shanter in 1953 pushed the button on the *All-Star Golf* idea. They were eighteen-hole contests between top pros. The first aired in the winter of 1954, between Sam Snead and Cary Middlecoff, and was played at Jemsek's Cog Hill Golf Course, in a western suburb of Chicago. Down the road it would be played on courses in Arizona, as well as famed Winged Foot GC and Oakland Hills CC. A total of 153 shows were produced between 1954 and 1961, at a rate of twenty-six a year. The winner of each match earned $1,000, the loser $500. The production values were not very high. Jemsek once said, "We were making home movies," but the shows gained a large audience and appeared for many years in re-reruns. And, it inspired such subsequent made-for-television programs as *Shell's Wonderful World of Golf*, the *CBS Golf Classic*, and *The World Series of Golf*.

First Live National Telecast of The US Open, **1954**. At Baltusrol GC.

First Live National Telecast of The Masters, **1956**.

First Live National Telecast of The PGA Championship, **1958**.

First Live International Telecast of The British Open, **1961**.

First Feature Movie on a Golf Theme, Follow the Sun, **1951**. A biopic, as we now say, of Ben Hogan. It appeared four years after the terrible highway accident he and his wife suffered and which almost took his life.

First Instructional Films for Commercial Release, **1931**. Bobby Jones made a series entitled *How I Play Golf* that appeared in movie houses around the country. They now appear occasionally on television (The Golf Channel, mainly).

Most Expensive Golf Book Sold at Retail, *The Golf Links of Scotland*, by Iain Macfarlane Lowe, $5,000. It is a book of photographs published in 2010.

***The Most Valuable Golf Book, The Goff*,** by Thomas Mathison. First published in 1743, with subsequent editions in 1763 and 1793, it is a collection of golf-themed poems. The Third Edition can be had for around $100,000.

First Book of Golf Fiction, *The Golficide*, by Van Passel Sutphen. Published in 1898, and like so much of golf fiction since, it is a murder mystery.

Most Popular Golf Instruction Book, *Harvey Penick's Little Redbook*, by Harvey Penick, with Bud Shrake. In its 19th printing to date, there are some 3.5 million copies in print.

First Noteworthy Golf Humor Book (according to Herbert Warren Wind), ***Hints on Golf*,** by Horace Hutchinson, 1886.

13 **ethnics**

▶ FIRSTS, MOSTS, AND LEASTS

While this category might seem irrelevant to the young people of the current generation, what country citizens came from and their ethnic background was for much of American history a definite point of interest. It was a reflection of a country built on the strength and diversity of immigration. There seems to be less interest in this among the current generation of young Americans, and that is probably a good thing. But to those of us of a different era, that aspect of American life is not entirely a thing of the past. And with that in mind we offer the following entries.

First African American to Play in the US Open, **John Shippen,** 1896. In fact, Shippen was part African and part Shinnecock Indian. But he was a man of color, and in America for quite a long while even just a little of it made him a "Negro." Thus, his entry in the championship was greeted poorly by the rest of the field, which was comprised entirely of white men, many natives of England and Scotland. When they declared they would not play in the tournament if Shippen were allowed to compete, the president of the USGA, Theodore Havemeyer, told them if that was the case the tournament would go on without them. No one withdrew.

Shippen, who was a caddie at the host club, Shinnecock Hills, on Long Island, New York, finished tied for fifth on rounds of 78–80 (it was a thirty-six-hole event; the championship did not go to seventy-two holes until the 1898 renewal).

Shippen made two more appearances in the championship, in 1899 (T24th) and 1900 (T25th). Alas, African Americans were subtly kept from competing in the national championship for many years afterward. The USGA did not bar them from entry, but because most of the qualifying sites it used were at private clubs, which did not allow blacks to play, very few were in the competition until the late 1940s.

First African American to Win a USGA Championship, **William Wright**, the 1959 US Publinks.

First African American's Participation in a PGA Tour Event, **1942**. From the mid-1930s into the early 1940s there had been an unwritten agreement between the PGA of America, which operated the Tour, and the sponsors of tour events, that African Americans—Negroes, in the terminology of the time—were not welcome to compete in their events. If entries were sent in they were not accepted. However, George S. May, the self-financed sponsor of two pro tournaments at his Tam O'Shanter CC, just outside Chicago, which offered the most lucrative purse money on the circuit, decided in 1942 to invite Negro professional and amateur golfers to try to qualify for his events. He had been lobbied by a black Chicago congressman to extend this invitation, but May also felt personally that it was not fair to exclude blacks from the opportunity to compete, and he readily complied.

That year, ten Negro professionals sought to qualify for the Tam O'Shanter All-American tournament, and to the surprise of many, seven did. That in itself was an accomplishment, because Negro golfers, professional or otherwise, had very limited access to public golf courses around the entire country, not just the South. This meant, of course, that the opportunity to play and practice was severely limited. Of those seven qualifiers, three made the thirty-six-hole cut, Calvin Searles, Howard Wheeler, and Zeke Hartsfield. None of them finished especially well, but the overall performance of the Negroes apparently shocked the PGA of America. The following year, at its annual meeting, a new codicil was included in the association's bylaws that only "Caucasians" would be accepted as members. That said, Negroes were now by PGA law unable to enter some 95 percent of the tournaments on the Tour because the PGA of America held jurisdiction over them and required membership in the association.

George May, as an independent sponsor, continued to invite Negroes to his tournaments, and in 1945 the Los Angeles Open sponsors did as well. Negros were also accepted in the Carling Tournament played in Canada and in the St. Paul Open in the late 1940s and into the 1950s. However, it wasn't until 1948 when black activist and golf professional, Bill Spiller, began a battle to expunge the Caucasians-only rule and open up full opportunities for men of his race to compete. His efforts, and those of others, bore fruit, finally, in 1958.

First African American to Win an Official PGA Tour Tournament, **Pete Brown**, the 1964 Waco Turner Open.

First African American to Win the US Amateur, **Tiger Woods,** 1994.

First African American to Win the US Open, **Tiger Woods**, 2000.

First African American to Win the Masters, **Tiger Woods**, 1997.

First African American to Win the British Open, **Tiger Woods,** 2000.

First African American to Win the PGA Championship, **Tiger Woods**, 1999.

First African American to Win the Players Championship, **Calvin Peete**, 1985.

First African American to Play in the Masters, **Lee Elder**, 1975.

First African American on USGA Executive Committee, **John Merchant**, 1992.

First Italian American to Win the US Open, British Open, Masters, and PGA Championship, **Gene Sarazen**, 1922, 1932, 1935, 1922, respectively.

First Italian American to Win the US Amateur, **Willie Turnesa**, 1938.

First Native American to Win on the PGA Tour, **Rod Curl**. A full-blooded Wintu, Curl played the Tour from 1969 through 1978. He finished in the top ten in forty-two events and won once, beating Jack Nicklaus by a stroke in the 1974 Colonial National Invitational.

First Jewish American Winner on PGA Tour, **Herman Barron**, 1946 Western Open.

First Jewish American Winner of the US Amateur, **Bruce Fleisher**, 1968.

First "Former" Jewish American Winner of the US Open, **Corey Pavin**, 1995. Pavin was born and raised in a Jewish family, but by the time he won the Open, at Shinnecock Hills GC, New York, he had adopted a Christian religion along Evangelical lines.

First Spanish American Winner of the PGA Championship and US Open, **Olin Dutra**, 1934, 1932, respectively.

First Hungarian American to Win the US Open, **Julius Boros**, who won it twice. Boros also won the 1969 PGA Championship, at age 48, and in all eighteen PGA Tour events. He also won events on the Senior PGA Tour.

First Mexican American to Win the US Open, the British Open, and the PGA Championship, **Lee Trevino**, 1968, 1971, 1974, respectively.

First Native Mexican to Win on the PGA Tour, **Victor Regalado**, 1974 Pleasant Valley Classic.

First Japanese American to Win on the PGA Tour, **David Ishii**, 1990 Hawaiian Open.

First German to Win the German Open, **Tiene Britz**, 1977.

First Frenchman to Win the French Open, **Arnaud Massy**, 1906.

First Spaniard to Win the Spanish Open, **Angel de La Torre**, 1916. De La Torre would emigrate to the United States and popularize a swing theory known as "Swing the Clubhead." His son, Manuel, became a fine golf teacher.

First Japanese to Compete in the United States, **R. Asaami and T. Miyamoto**. Miyamoto teed it up in the 1922 National Match-Play Championship, at Lake Merced CC, in San Francisco.

First American to Win the Portugese Open, **Hal Underwood**, 1975.

First American to Win the Spanish Open, **Arnold Palmer**, 1975.

First American to Win the Italian Open, **Billy Casper**, 1975.

First American to Win the French Open, **Walter Hagen**, 1920.

First American to Win the Scandinavian Open, **George Burns**, 1975.

First American to Win the Irish Open, Ben Crenshaw, 1976.

First American to Win the German Open, Corey Pavin, 1983.

First Famous American Golfer to "Anglicize" His Last Name, **Gene Sarazen**. He was born Eugenio Saraceni, the son of immigrant Italians. Sarazen said Saraceni sounded more like a violin player than a golfer, and while his alteration doesn't particularly sound it he was reflecting an early-twentieth-century tradition among many "ethnic" Americans—Italians, Jews, Poles, etc.—to make their names more "American." Or, less ethnic. Others in golf who followed that pattern were Doug Ford, winner of a Masters and PGA, who was born Fortinacci; and Billy Burke, winner of the 1931 US Open, who was born Burkowski.

14 **nevers**

Great Players Who Never Won an Amateur Tournament, **John McDermott, Walter Hagen, Gene Sarazen, Ben Hogan, Jimmy Demaret, Jack Burke Jr., Sam Snead, Lee Trevino, Gary Player, Billy Casper, Harry Vardon, Ted Ray, and Seve Ballesteros.**

Legendary Champion Who Never Crossed Swilcan Bridge at St. Andrews Old Course, **Ben Hogan.** It has become a kind of rite of retirement for golf champions to make a photographed farewell from the center of this small, slightly arched stone bridge that crosses a narrow burn midway down the 18th fairway of golf's "home" course. Of course, Hogan had passed before the ritual began, but Hogan never saw St. Andrews under any circumstances, and apparently didn't care.

Greatest Champion Who Never Won the PGA Championship, **Arnold Palmer.**

Greatest Champion Ever to Never Win the US Open, **Sam Snead.**

Best Player to Never Win a Major, **Harry Cooper.**

A Naturalized American Citizen Has Never Played on a US Ryder Cup Team. As noted earlier, driving force behind the American interest in the Ryder Cup Matches was to show off the competence of American-born pros. Into the 1920s many private golf clubs in the

United States were hiring British and Scottish born head pros on the grounds that coming from the birthplace of golf they were best qualified for the jobs. The PGA of America felt that if the American-born pros defeated the Brits/Scots in the Matches, it would indicate they had the credentials to head up pro shops. Therefore, the PGA of America decreed that to be eligible for the American team a player had to be born in the United States. The idea worked, because the American teams did well from the start. However, because of this rule such outstanding players as Tommy Armour and Harry Cooper, who were born in Great Britain but became citizens of and made their careers in the United States, never played Ryder Cup golf. The rule was contrary to the immigrant history of the United States, and it was finally modified in 2000. Now, anyone born abroad of American parents, or who becomes an American citizen before his eighteenth birthday, is eligible for the American team. To date, no one has come up with those credentials.

Winston Churchill is often credited with originating one of golf's most famous, and literate aphorisms, to wit, "Golf is a game in which a small ball is propelled into a small hole with implements singularly unsuited to the task." He may have used the line, but he **Never** originated it. In fact, it was the work (or lyricism, if you please) of Lord Arthur James Balfour, a prime minister of England at the turn of the twentieth century, who loved golf and wrote about it in Badminton's volume on golf (1890). He obviously couldn't play very well, so his wonderful description of the game was well earned.

No One Has Ever Won a Major Championship on His/Her Birthday.

There has Never been an official or unofficial committee or even a random group of persons standing around a bar in a locker room to signify or determine what is a "major" championship. The designation, which carries enormous respect for golfers who win one, not to mention a potentially excellent financial profit, has simply arisen. It gained purchase in golf in the late 1950s and is made up of four tournaments, three of which, by my estimation, have a certain legitimacy. The US and British Opens are conducted by the two of the most influential administrative bodies in the game—the Royal & Ancient Golf Club of St. Andrews and the United States Golf Association. As such, their premier competitions, the Opens, bring together the best golfers in the world to play on top-drawer tests of the game, but the R&A and USGA stand for the game itself and the millions who play it and abide by the rules of golf that both organizations oversee. The PGA Championship is produced by the PGA of America, which represents thousands of golf professionals and, in this respect, plays an important role in the ongoing development of the interest in and the growth of golf. The fourth "major" is the Masters tournament, which by the above criteria has the least claim on the designation. It represents a very small, elite group of wealthy members of a very private golf club that, unlike the other three organizations, makes a financial profit from their tournament that does not find its way back into real development and growth of golf.

Jack Nicklaus, from Ohio, **Never won the Ohio State Amateur championship**, while *Arnold Palmer,* from Pennsylvania, **Never won the Pennsylvania Amateur championship**. But Palmer twice won the Ohio State Amateur. Go figure.

Well into his third hour of practice on the range at Pebble Beach during the week of a 2011 Senior PGA Tour event, Tom Kite, a prodigious, seemingly tireless ball-beater, was asked by a friend passing by what he (Kite) would do if they ever ran out of balls. Kite's reply was delivered as an article of faith—*"They will Never run out of balls."*

abbreviations

A	amateur
AIA	Association of Intercollegiate Athletics for Women
CC	Country Club
DQ	disqualified
E	even par
GC	Golf Club
GL	Golf Links
mc	missed cut
NCAA	National Collegiate Athletic Association
R&A	Royal & Ancient Golf Society of St. Andrews
T	tie
USF&G Classic	United States Fidelity and Guaranty Company Classic
USGA	United States Golf Association
wd	withdrew

reader's personal firsts, mosts, leasts, & nevers

FIRST TIME I BROKE 100

when _____

where _____

score _____

FIRST TIME I BROKE 90

when _____

where _____

score _____

FIRST TIME I BROKE 80

when _____

where _____

score _____

FIRST HOLE IN ONE

when _____

where _____

length of hole _____

club used _____

make of ball used _____

MOST HOLES PLAYED IN ONE DAY

when _____

where _____

scores _____

MOST BIRDIES/PAR MADE IN SINGLE ROUND

when _____

where _____

total score for round _____

_____

LEAST NUMBER OF PUTTS IN A SINGLE ROUND

when _____

where _____

total score for round _____

_____

LEAST NUMBER OF BALLS LOST IN ROUND

NEVER

threw a club in anger _____

cursed after missing a short putt

---

ate a hotdog with everything on it between nines _____

refused to accept a gimme putt

---

hit a better/worse shot with a mulligan